All About Aquariums

The photos on the following pages are by Vince Serbin: 10, 13, 21, 23, 27, 29, 30, 31, 32, 42, 47, 51, 54, 57, 60, 64, 65, 66, 67, 95, 97, 99, 103, 104, 115.

Distributed in the U.S. by T.F.H. Publications, Inc., 211 West Sylvania Avenue, PO Box 427, Neptune, NJ 07753; in England by T.F.H. (Gt. Britain) Ltd., 13 Nutley Lane, Reigate, Surrey; in Canada to the pet trade by Rolf C. Hagen Ltd., 3225 Sartelon Street, Montreal 382, Quebec; in Canada to the book trade by H & L Pet Supplies, Inc., 27 Kingston Crescent, Kitchener, Ontario N28 2T6; in Southeast Asia by Y.W. Ong, 9 Lorong 36 Geylang, Singapore 14; in Australia and the South Pacific by Pet Imports Pty. Ltd., P.O. Box 149, Brookvale 2100, N.S.W. Australia; in South Africa by Valid Agencies, P.O. Box 51901, Randburg 2125 South Africa. Published by T.F.H. Publications, Inc., Ltd., the British Crown Colony of Hong Kong.

All About Aquariums

A Book for Beginners, with Step-by-Step Information on Selecting, Lighting, Heating, Filtering, Planting and Setting Up an Aquarium.

By Earl Schneider

To my mother —
who suffered fish in the bathtub.

TABLE OF CONTENTS

Aquarium Dimensions and Equivalent Capacities in (U.S.) Gallons

Width Inches	Length Inches	Height Inches	Capacity
6	10	8	2 Gal.
7	12	9	3 Gal.
8	14	10	5 Gal.
8	16	10	$5\frac{1}{2}$ Gal.
9	18	11	8 Gal.
10	20	12	10 Gal.
10	20	14	12 Gal.
10	20	16	$13\frac{1}{2}$ Gal.
8	24	12	10 Gal.
8	24	14	12 Gal.
8	24	16	$13\frac{1}{2}$ Gal.
12	24	12	15 Gal.
12	24	14	17 Gal.
12	24	16	20 Gal.
12	30	12	20 Gal.
12	30	14	23 Gal.
12	30	16	26 Gal.
12	30	18	29 Gal.
12	36	16	30 Gal.
12	36	18	34 Gal.
14	36	16	35 Gal.
14	36	18	39 Gal.
16	36	18	42 Gal.
18	36	18	50 Gal.

CHAPTER I

SELECTING YOUR AQU`RIUM

LET'S IMAGINE YOU HAVE BECOME INTERESTED in tropical fishes. There are a lot of questions on your mind. You aren't quite sure that you know enough about an aquarium to set one up properly. Perhaps you think it is beyond your means. You are puzzled . . . you just don't know whether to go ahead with it.

The best way to acquire information about aquariums is to talk with well-informed dealers. Then talk with hobbyists who are having success with tropical fishes and aquariums. Enlarge your fund of information by comparing experiences with them and by reading helpful books and magazines such as *Tropical Fish Hobbyist* on the subject.

This book that you are holding can be a big help to you if you are a beginner. It answers most of the questions that you are sure to be asking yourself. For example:

How expensive is it to start?

A start can be made with a small aquarium, inexpensive fishes, and a minimum of equipment for from $25. to $35. I have also seen people start off with a large aquarium, expensive equipment, and fishes, paying about $400 for the initial investment. In either case, the purchaser was satisfied because he got what he wanted and bought within his means. If you cannot afford a large aquarium, by all means start with a small one. You can have just as much fun.

What information should I have on aquarium keeping?

There are certain basic rules which should be learned.

Each person has individual problems. It is not necessary to learn everything in order to keep an aquarium. The fact that millions of people have kept and are keeping aquariums throughout the world is in itself proof that it is not too difficult for the average person to learn in limited time.

What size aquarium should I start with?

The first criterion usually is price. Don't spend more than you can comfortably afford. I would suggest that the beginner select a 10- to 20-gallon aquarium for a start. A 10-gallon aquarium measures, in inches, 20Lx10Wx12H. A 20-gallon tank is 24Lx12Wx16H. The 20-gallon tank is also made in a longer, lower shape, measuring 30Lx12Wx 12H. I consider these ideal intermediate sizes for a beginner. They are not too expensive, and they are the easiest to set up and care for. To estimate the gallon capacity of a tank, multiply the width by the length by the height in inches and divide by 231.*

How about starting off with a round bowl?

As a main aquarium, the round bowl is sadly deficient. The largest fish globe made today in a standard size holds 2 gallons when filled to the brim. Because the sides of a fish bowl are curved, it is most efficient when filled only to its widest part. This gives you a maximum of water surface exposed to the air but reduces the capacity of the bowl to $1\frac{1}{2}$ gallons of water. (Air surface and its relationship to the life of the fish will come up again.) This is just not enough water to maintain a satisfactory aquarium.

Why not start with a small aquarium?

Primarily because a small tank is limited in its capacity and can very easily be overstocked. Overcrowding, like any other excess, leads to trouble. A conscientious dealer will warn about overcrowding when you are buying too many fishes. Get his advice by telling him the size of your tank and how many fishes you already have in it.

Incidentally, today the average cost of a 5-gallon

*See chart showing dimensions and capacity on page 6.

aquarium is only a couple of dollars less than a 10-gallon aquarium. In fact the cost of the equipment will run about the same to outfit a 5-gallon aquarium as it would for a 10-gallon aquarium. The reason for this is that most of the equipment you will need for the 5-gallon aquarium is the same used for the 10-gallon aquarium. Some of the equipment may cost more for the 5-gallon aquarium if it is not a popular item that is mass produced. Gallon for gallon, a small tank costs more than a large one. Therefore buying a very small tank is not really economical at all.

There are two types of stands available in most pet shops, wrought iron and wood. You will find the iron stands to be less expensive, although many of the wooden stands are competitively priced. The iron stands are open on all sides, while many of the wooden models are enclosed to give a cabinet-like appearance with doors in front.

How about starting with a really big tank?

It is a good idea if you can afford it. The equipment required is somewhat more expensive, requiring heavier-duty heating and filtering units than the smaller, average-size tank. But remember that if something goes wrong due to mishandling, a change often becomes necessary. And it is quite a chore to change all the water and clean the gravel in a 40- or 50-gallon tank.

A large tank has certain decided advantages. A large number of fishes can be kept without overcrowding, and they will usually grow better than when kept in smaller confines. There are several species of fishes which tend to be pugnacious when crowded into a small aquarium. Many of these same fishes are quite peaceful when given more "fin room." Scenically, an artistic person can really "let himself go" with a large aquarium. A little imagination can transform a large aquarium into an enchanting underwater garden, with grottoes and mountains, valleys, and even lawns. A lovely little plant, Micro-sagittaria, never grows more than an inch or so high. Planted toward the front of an aquarium, it soon covers the bottom with a luxuriant green lawn. Best of all, it requires no mowing!

A 20-gallon aquarium is an excellent size for a first aquarium. It is large enough to aquascape with driftwood, plants and ornaments. Placed on a cabinet-style wooden stand, your aquarium will become a focal point in your home or office.

Will changing the water make my tank leak?

Not if the change is made properly. Never pick up a tank and pour out the water, never move a full tank, and never pick up a tank by the upper rim. Always siphon out as much water as possible before moving the tank. Pick the tank up from the bottom and move it as carefully as possible.

I would like to set a large tank between two rooms. It would have to be very tall and narrow. Is this practical?

Try to avoid tall, narrow tanks whenever possible. Oxygen, which will be discussed in another chapter, is absorbed primarily at the surface. The narrow tank limits the number of fishes which can be kept to the area of exposed surface regardless of the depth of the water. As a matter of fact, if the depth of the water is too great in relation to the amount of surface, a concentration of carbon dioxide and other poisonous materials could accumulate in the lower areas and prevent any fishes from living there. It is not unusual in high tanks to see the inhabitants frequenting only the upper stratum and descending to the bottom only briefly to pick up a bit of food.

As a general rule, it is practical to have the combined length and width of the aquarium at least three times the height. The combined length and width should never be less than twice the height.

Why should so much consideration be given to the tank?

I consider the tank to be the cornerstone of the aquarium hobby. It is the foundation on which to build. All the equipment is selected to be suitable for the aquarium. It is even a good idea to select fishes that are most suitable to the type aquarium you have chosen.

Where should the tank be placed?

First of all, we must consider what the tank is to stand on. Water is quite heavy—8.3 pounds per U.S. gallon. Thus a 15-gallon tank weighs about 125 pounds. This is certainly no weight for a delicate end table to support. The base for a tank must be a sturdy one—flat and level. Any projections, tilt, or unsteadiness may cause leakage. The location should be a fairly permanent one. Tanks cannot be moved readily. Also, the height must be considered. It should be high enough to be seen standing up and low enough to be viewed comfortably while sitting down. An ideal height for a stand is 30″ to 36″.

Stands expressly designed for supporting aquaria are available. Most of these are equipped with a shelf which can be used for an auxiliary tank or for equipment. The artistically inclined often put plants on the shelf and train ivy up the legs to afford an exotic touch. These stands have a flat top, open in the center, with just a rim around the edge to support the tank. The center is left open so that water, which may accidentally drip, will not run under and accumulate below the tank. The outside rim which supports the tank only along the four edges is perfectly satisfactory.

When the stand rests on a rug or linoleum, furniture coasters should be used to prevent damage. Some buyers are surprised to see that there is no lip around a stand to prevent sliding. Because of a tank's construction, all of the weight and pressure are directed straight down, and it would require a very heavy shove to dislodge a tank. In fact, a shove heavy enough to move a full tank is more likely to break the tank before moving it. The moral of the story is: don't shove a full tank.

Think twice before putting a tank on an expensive piece of highly polished furniture. Working around an aquarium, water is often spilled, and tank water is injurious to polished surfaces unless it is wiped up immediately. Surfaces which heat up, such as television cabinets, may cause the cement to soften. Several layers of asbestos under the tank will prevent this. A table-top stand has recently become available. This is approximately 4″ high and is designed for holding tanks on furniture.

This aquarium is aquascaped with plastic plants, gravel, rocks and a natural scene background. The wrought iron stand is less expensive than a cabinet stand and serves the same purpose.

Is a radiator a good stand?

Definitely not. Many people put their tanks on or near radiators under the mistaken impression that the heat will be beneficial. Heating will be discussed in Chapter 3, but it should be noted here that the heat of a radiator, being unregulated, may actually be harmful rather than beneficial. The heat of the radiator may also melt the cement. If a location over a radiator is the only place available, build a raised platform and line it with asbestos or some other good insulating material.

I would like to build a tank into a bookcase or some other article of furniture. Is it practical?

Very much so. A built-in aquarium makes a most attractive display. An aquarium may also be built into a

wall, or in a wall between two rooms. Each job presents its
own problems, but there are certain things that apply
to all of them.

A tank expands slightly when it is filled, so never fit a
tank snugly into a space. Always allow at least $\frac{1}{2}''$ for
expansion on each side. When the tank is fitted into a
closed object, keep evaporation in mind. Line the sides
and top with a waterproof material or non-toxic waterproof paint, and allow adequate ventilation.

When building a tank into an outside wall, remember
that the back of the compartment may become quite cold
during the winter and hot during the summer—insulate it.
Always allow easy accessibility for frequent chores such
as feeding, siphoning, glass cleaning, etc. At least a 6-inch
span should be allowed above the aquarium to permit
entry of a hand.

A fluorescent light (a multi-spectrum bulb is best) is
preferable to an incandescent one in an enclosed place.
The heat given off by an incandescent light is a definite
drawback, particularly during the warmer months. Always
make provision so that the tank can be removed when
necessary without destroying the piece of furniture. When
using a motor-driven pump in the same compartment
with the tank, allow adequate ventilation for it, because
motor-driven pumps give off quite a bit of heat.

A hinged frame which conceals the frame of the aquarium can greatly enhance its appearance. It gives the
aquarium a picturelike quality. Frequently a wall installation is made in a living-room wall which is next to a closet.
A shelf is built in the closet which supports the tank against
an opening cut into the viewing-room wall. All servicing
can then be done from the rear.

Can an aquarium be kept in offices and showrooms which are closed for weekends and holidays?

All other things being equal, the care and maintenance
of an aquarium in an office or showroom is very little
different from the care required in a home. Heat and electricity, however, must be maintained over the weekends.

It is impossible to maintain tropical aquaria without constant proper heating. The cold of a winter weekend, without electricity to operate the heater, would kill the fishes.

In schools and offices where electricity is not turned off, it is best to leave a light burning over the aquarium during weekends, so that the plants can perform their functions adequately. Check all the equipment carefully. Feed the fishes a normal meal—nothing extra, and do the same thing upon returning. Fishes can manage quite some time without food.

CHAPTER II

LIGHT AND YOUR AQUARIUM

ALL LIFE, AS WE KNOW IT, IS AFFECTED BY LIGHT. Under the influence of sunlight, plants and only plants have the ability to manufacture their own food. These green plants combine water and carbon dioxide to form sugars in a process known as "photosynthesis."

During this process, free oxygen is released in excess of that used by the plant for respiration. This occurs only under the influence of bright light. At other times the plant breathes normally, consuming oxygen and giving off carbon dioxide. Photosynthesis occurs only when the plant in light is healthy and growing.

Light, then, is essential to your aquarium so that the plants will grow properly and give off oxygen and consume carbon dioxide. The "wonder material" that regulates the food manufacturing process is chlorophyll—the material that gives plants their green color.

Do plants supply all the oxygen that fishes require in an aquarium?

There is a good deal of controversy concerning the amount of oxygen that the plants actually supply for fishes to use.

It should be remembered that water can dissolve only a certain amount of oxygen; any excess oxygen is therefore released at the surface. It is not stored in the water for later use as the fishes require it. The temperature of the water is also an influencing factor; the warmer the water, the smaller the percentage of dissolved oxygen it can hold.

The whole subject is quite a complicated one and far beyond the scope of this book. However, certain relationships seem pretty definitely established as true. Plants, as oxygenators, are certainly inferior to the natural interchange of gases that takes place between the atmosphere

Planting arranged for beauty and best use of front light.

and water at the water's surface. Here carbon dioxide is released and oxygen is taken into the water. The process can be hastened by bubbling a stream of air through the water. This tends to agitate the water and increase the area exposed to the surface in proportion to the amount of circulation engendered. Manual stirring of the water serves the same purpose, but it is not so convenient a method as the mechanical one.

The greater the area of the exposed-to-air water surface, the faster oxygen will be taken in and carbon dioxide released. That is the reason for the emphasis put on tank shapes in the previous chapter. The greater the air surface, the more fishes can be kept in a given volume of water. You do not really increase the capacity of the tank to hold fishes simply by raising the height of the water in the tank. You must also increase the other dimensions in proportion.

Are plants really necessary in an aquarium?

Probably the same number of fishes could be maintained in a bare aquarium as in one with plants. Then, you may ask, why bother with plants? Well, plants serve many functions besides the disputed one of oxygenating. The principal function is an esthetic one: there would not be much beauty to a tank without plants. They provide an excellent background against which your colorful fishes will display themselves to best advantage. Other plant functions are listed on page 73.

Do fishes require light?

Not nearly so much as the plants do. A dim light is sufficient for fishes—usually just enough for them to see food. Very few fishes will eat in the dark. An exception is the Catfish; Catfishes, as a group, are largely nocturnal in their activities.

When no light reaches the tank, a great change comes over the fishes. Switch a light on suddenly after a protracted period of darkness and you will find most fishes in your tank are motionless. With few exceptions you will find that their color has faded. Such fishes as the brilliant red-and-green Neon fade to a white and light pink. Many fishes, you will notice, are lying on the bottom of the tank.

It should also be remembered that it takes some time for most fishes to adjust to a sudden light. If they are disturbed before their eyes have adjusted, they dash blindly about, even leaping out of the water. It is useless to feed them at this time, because they cannot see the food.

On the other hand, constant light seems to do no harm. Fishes in aquaria under constant light appear to live just as well as those that have alternate periods of darkness and light. The breeding cycle of many animals is controlled by the increasing and decreasing of the number of daylight hours as the seasons change. But very little work has been done with fishes in this field. What little has been done shows that light is a definite factor in the breeding of some, but not all, fishes. Recently published experiments conducted with the young of certain marine fishes indicate that the fish will grow more vigorously when given a period of darkness in which to rest. How this affects the total longevity of the fish is not known.

How much light do plants require?

There is no hard-and-fast rule governing this. It varies with the type of light, intensity of light, depth of water, kind of plant, the distance the light is from the water surface, and the amount of daylight that reaches the tank. Usually, if the tank is kept in a shaded area of a room, you should provide some artificial light in order to supply what the plants need. Lighting from a reflector which can be regulated is covered later.

What is the best way to light an aquarium?

Aquaria should be lighted from the front and the top. The rays of the light should be directed down and back toward the rear, bottom. They should be directed away from the viewer's eyes, striking the fishes directly to reveal their beauty. Light coming from the rear tends to silhouette the fish and to conceal refractive colors.

As a general rule, eight to ten hours of light a day, utilizing the wattages given, will result in satisfactory plant growth. Larger wattages may be used for lesser periods of time, and smaller wattages for greater. That there is a point of diminishing returns is obvious. Too low a wattage will not penetrate a depth of water; too high a wattage may overheat the upper layer of the water. Observation over a period of time will determine the most satisfactory wattage to use and the proper period of time to keep the lights on.

The most satisfactory arrangement is one that keeps the

plants healthy and the algae growth down to a minimum. Should the plants start to deteriorate, usually more light is required; that is, higher wattages or a longer period of illumination.

Excessive growth of algae usually indicates too much light and, possibly, an excess of decomposing organic matter. The remedy, usually, is to decrease the amount of illumination and to siphon off all excess food and foreign matter. A certain amount of algae is bound to form even under ideal conditions. But you can keep this minimal growth in check by scraping and by using scavengers. You should be most concerned with the wild, seemingly uncontrollable growth that coats the rocks and plants and turns the water green.

The control and removal of algae and excess food will be discussed in subsequent chapters.

Is there much danger of a short circuit from wet wires?

The practical danger is very slight. In all the years that I have been around aquariums I have yet to hear of anyone suffering a serious shock. All wiring is rubber or plastic coated. The little brackets which hold the sockets in place are one of the greatest drawbacks in the construction of reflectors. Some manufacturers fail to make these of rust-proof materials. Exposed to constant moisture, they eventually rust through, and it is difficult to replace them. When possible, try to get brass or stainless steel fittings to hold the sockets. If your fittings start to rust, clean them thoroughly with a good rust remover, then paint them with a good quality spar varnish after they dry. A switch should be built into the reflector. If you have one without a switch, a line switch is easy to obtain and install. It is dangerous and inconvenient to keep pulling out and replacing the plug when turning the light on and off.

Is the use of colored bulbs advisable?

Certain colors, although pretty to see, actually inhibit the growth of plants. The warmer tones at the red end of the spectrum are the most satisfactory for plant stimula-

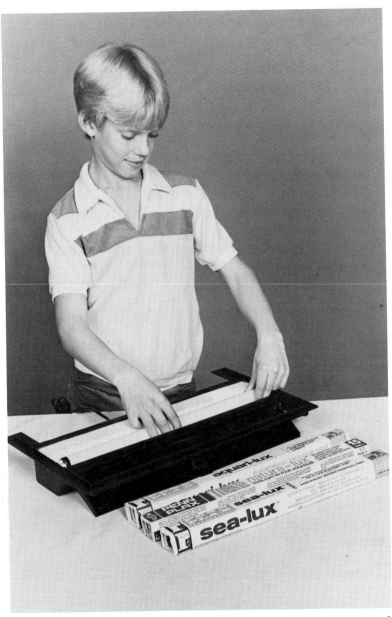

Several types of lighting tubes are available to imitate various types of natural light.

tion. Blue colors are the least helpful. The most practical are the uncoated clear glass bulbs which have a long filament. Although there are a number of inexpensive bulbs on the market which have short filaments, actual tests have proven them to be less effective than the long in stimulating plant growth. Any coating on a bulb must of necessity diminish the amount of light reaching the plants and thus decrease the effectiveness of the bulb.

Should incandescent or fluorescent light be used?

Some reflectors are fitted with sockets for a fluorescent tube instead of incandescent bulbs. There is a good deal of controversy concerning the relative merits of the two systems. Experiments conducted by Dr. C. W. Coates at the New York Aquarium indicated that a combination of both incandescent and fluorescent lighting gives the most satisfactory results. His experiments also showed that light, in order to be satisfactory, must be directed from above. Light from the side has a greatly decreased value.

It is impractical for the average hobbyist with a small or medium aquarium to use both types of light, however. Properly used, either will give a satisfactory growth to the average aquarium plant, although it may not necessarily give maximum growth.

The initial outlay for a fluorescent fixture is slightly higher than that for an incandescent. This is offset by the fact that a fluorescent bulb consumes much less current. Also, the higher cost of a replacement tube for a fluorescent is balanced by its longer life. In addition, fluorescent fixtures give a stronger, more even light, and they do not heat up the aquarium. This is particularly important during the summer, when preventing any increase in the already high water temperature and yet supplying enough light for the plants can be a problem. When using a fluorescent, the red end of the spectrum should be favored for color because it is the most beneficial. White, cold white, and daylight bulbs are not so satisfactory as warm tints, warm tones, or deluxe warm whites.

Full hoods are available with incandescent or fluorescent fixtures. This fluorescent hood is a woodgrain style matching the trim on the aquarium.

How long should a fluorescent burn?

As with an incandescent, the time required to obtain results is extremely variable. In general it should burn two to three times as long as an incandescent reflector under comparable circumstances.

For tanks of 20 to 30 gallons in capacity, the standard reflector holds a 20-watt bulb. It is frequently necessary to burn a bulb of this size twenty-four hours a day in order to achieve satisfactory plant growth. For smaller tanks, sixteen to twenty hours of light a day is usually necessary. If it is inconvenient to turn the light on and off at the time necessary to provide the proper illumination, it is perfectly satisfactory to burn the light twelve hours one day and twenty four hours on alternate days.

One of the most satisfactory tanks I had experience with was a 27-gallon aquarium owned by a businessman. It measured 36 inches long by 12 inches wide by 14 inches high, and was equipped with a 20-watt warm-white fluorescent fixture which burned continually. The plant and fish growth in that tank was phenomenal. Ambulia, Amazon Sword Plants, *Hygrophila,* and *Cryptocoryne* of different species grew in profusion. Magnificent fish luxuriated among the dense growth. No attention was given to the tank other than feeding and replacing water lost through evaporation. Every month a pet shop owner was called in to siphon the bottom clean, and to remove a pailful of excess plant growth.

Is it necessary for a tank to get daylight?

No; as a matter of fact, daylight, being difficult to control, frequently makes it difficult to balance a tank properly. A location well away from the light is perfectly satisfactory. An aquarium frequently serves a dual purpose as a lamp in a dark vestibule or corner. Should it be desirable to keep an aquarium near a window, do not be deterred by the foregoing, since there are ways of controlling daylight to make it suit your purpose. A northern exposure is best, though for second choice a western exposure is preferable for a tank located near a window.

Is sunlight necessary to plant and fish life?

For all practical purposes, sunlight is unnecessary to an aquarium. Not only is it unnecessary, but it can actually be dangerous and harmful if the aquarium is exposed to it to excess. The difficulty with sunlight is that it is hard to control, and its occurrence is impossible to predict. A little sunlight for an aquarium situated in a window may be beneficial during the colder months when the rays are weak. Those same rays may become a menace during the warmer months of the year, even cooking the fishes and plants in extreme cases. What usually happens is that the best heat of the sun warms the aquarium considerably during the day. At night there is a sharp drop in temperature. Most tropicals are mildly tolerant of a minor temperature change which does not occur too often. When it is both sharp and frequent, it usually leads to complications and disease.

Besides the heat problem, the strong rays of direct sunlight frequently trigger the growth of microscopic plants known as algae. Although the discussion of algae properly belongs in the section under plants, I feel that it is so intimately connected with the light problem that it is best discussed here.

What are algae?

According to the dictionary, algae are "A group of plants that have chlorophyll but do not have true roots, stems, or leaves. Some algae are small single cells and form scum on rocks; others, such as various seaweeds, are very large."

We are concerned in the aquarium with the minute and, primarily, single-cell forms of algae. The spores of many of them are extremely hardy, can resist drying and freezing, and may be air-borne. A completely sterile aquarium, unless it is sealed shut, can develop the algal growth from spores deposited in it through the air. A pond that dries up every year develops algae when the rains refill it and the sun warms and lights it.

The most common form found in the aquarium is the fuzzy alga that forms on the glass under the reflector, or wherever light strikes the tank. More objectionable are the slime algae that form slick sheets on the glass, rocks, and plants. Most dangerous are the bright blue-green algae that may be poisonous.

Not so serious, but quite annoying, are the thread algae which blanket the bottom and rocks. Then there is "green water," which is simply an uncontrolled growth of free-floating algae. In extreme cases this can become so thick that aquarium inhabitants only an inch away from the glass are invisible.

Many aquarists cultivate aquaria of "green water," believing that it has great therapeutic value. Many cures are attributed to the simple art of placing a fish in a tank of "green water" for several weeks. Nevertheless, "green water" of all algae is potentially the most dangerous to fishes. During the warmer months the oxygen content of the aquarium is at its lowest. Should the algae causing the "green water" be deprived of light, even for only a few hours, they start a chain reaction in which the algae use up all the available oxygen in respiration. Deprived of oxygen, the algae start to die. Normally, the lower areas are first affected, as they are farthest from the surface where oxygen enters. Being dead, the tiny plants decompose rapidly in the warm water. Decomposition also uses up oxygen and gives off carbon dioxide. This hastens the process, and a tank of "green water" can thus become an odorous mass of rotting algae within a few hours.

It is best to eliminate "green water" before the growth becomes too heavy. Usually this can be done by cutting down the amount of light. This dimming of the light should be done gradually. Cutting off all the light at once can cause the algae to die suddenly, with the resultant decomposition mentioned before.

Placing a large quantity of *Daphnia* (small water crustaceans), which feed on "green water," in the tank for a few days will also usually clear it up. However, the fishes must be removed or they will eat the *Daphnia*. They can be replaced to clear up the *Daphnia* after the latter have done their job.

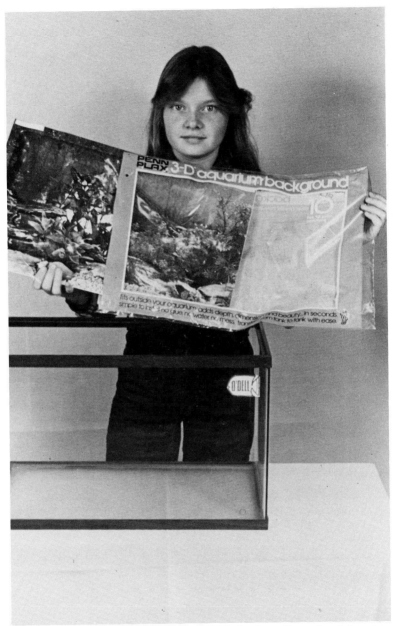

Natural scenery backgrounds are available in three-dimensional forms to add beauty and depth to your aquarium.

Fresh-water mussels will also eliminate "green water." The difficulty is that once they have done the job, they may starve to death and pollute the tank. The quickest method is to dissolve one grain of potassium permanganate by weight to every gallon of aquarium water. This turns the water pink or brown but clears it in a few days. This treatment is also effective for a grayish cloud caused by excess bacterial activity. Should the fishes show any distress by hanging at the surface of the water after treatment, change one-third to one-half of the water.

Keeping an aquarium clean will help control algae by depriving them of one of their basic foods—the CO_2 caused by decomposition.

Changing all or part of the water is worse than useless. Fresh water acts as a stimulant and actually increases the growth of algae.

The other algae mentioned—thread, blanket, and filament—will all yield to decreased light. Siphoning can remove much of the blanket algae. *Plecostomus* catfish and snails will eat the filamentous types. A fork can be used to entangle and uproot thread algae, while a stiff brush will remove it from rocks and ornaments.

What are the brown algae?

Occasionally, when there is too little light, and usually in the presence of decaying matter, a brown slime forms on the glass. This, too, is an alga; the brown color is due to the color of its spores. Scraping, Sucker-mouthed Catfish, and snails will remove it, although the long-term cure is to eliminate the cause. Increase the amount of light and clean the tank for a sure remedy.

The only convenient location for my tank is in a sunny window. What can I do?

By painting the back a light color and shading the top of the tank you can considerably mitigate the effects of the direct sunlight. Heavy algae growth forming on the back of the tank should not be removed. Although they will not cut down the heat, they will diminish the glare.

A floating plant such as *Riccia* or *Salvinia* can be used on the surface. Thin this out as it multiplies, because the upper layers, when too heavy, can smother and kill the lower ones. Floating plants do not materially affect the interchange of gases at the surface.

Is ordinary daylight harmful?

Daylight or indirect sunlight, being so much less intense than direct sunlight, is easier to control and more beneficial. Natural light must be taken into account when computing the length of time the reflector should be kept lighted. The more natural light a tank receives the less artificial light it requires, and vice versa.

What is the difference between a hood and a reflector?

A reflector is usually only $3\frac{1}{2}$ or 4 inches wide and covers only the front few inches of the aquarium. A hood covers the entire tank. Usually, although not always, the sockets in a hood are set in the center.

The hood, which requires more material and labor to make, is more expensive. It offers the advantage of protecting the tank from dirt and dust and preventing excessive evaporation.

Like full hood reflectors, strip reflectors also are available with either fluorescent or incandescent fixtures. This incandescent reflector has a two-bulb fixture and can accommodate clear or colored bulbs.

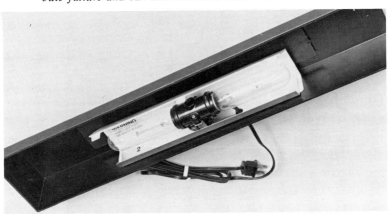

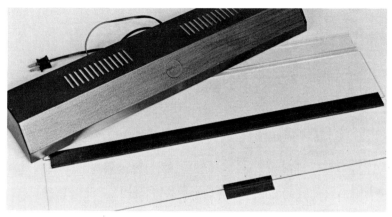

A glass cover and a strip reflector are sufficient for covering and lighting your aquarium.

This full hood is constructed of a light-weight unbreakable plastic. The front piece is hinged so that you can easily feed your fish.

What is a cover glass and how does it fit?

A cover glass is an aquarium cover. It is best made of light plate glass so as to be more break-resistant. When used with a reflector, the glass should start from just behind the reflector and cover the balance of the tank. Under no circumstance should the cover glass be extended under the incandescent reflector. The heat of the bulbs is likely to crack the glass. Also, the glass coming between the light and the tank may filter out a good deal of the

Outside filters are easy to use and most efficient. By placing the filter outside the aquarium you have more room in the aquarium for aquascaping.

Now available are digital thermometers that are placed on the outside glass of an aquarium. These thermometers are even more accurate than most that are placed inside the aquarium.

light and retard plant growth. With a hood, no cover glass is necessary.

The rear corners of the cover glass may be cut out for a heater and/or filter. There are clips and handles available which can be fastened in place to suspend the cover glass inside and just below the rim, rather than having it rest on the rim of the tank. These are helpful because they prevent moisture from gathering between the glass and tank rim and corroding it.

When neither reflector nor hood is used, a cover glass should protect the whole aquarium.

Why use a cover glass?

The functions of a cover glass are many. It helps regulate the temperature, prevents fishes from jumping out, reduces evaporation, keeps out dust and dirt, and also keeps out inquisitive fingers and paws!

For a tank kept in a sunny or extremely light location, the cover may be of translucent glass to cut down the glare.

Should I depend on my reflector to heat the aquarium?

Definitely not! For proper aquarium heating you need a source of heat that can be regulated. This will be discussed fully in the chapter on heating.

The heat given off by the reflector is incidental. Most people turn their reflectors on in the evening when the house is at its warmest and turn it off when they go to bed. Should they be dependent solely on the reflector for heat regulation this would result in the tank temperature being at its peak during the evening and plunging rapidly down during the night, when the light and usually the central heating system are both turned off. This could be disastrous. Unless you are prepared to keep a close watch on your tank thermometer, turning on the light as the temperature drops and turning it off when the heat rises, you cannot depend on the reflector. Actually, you would be turning yourself into a thermostat. It is much more practical to buy one.

CHAPTER III

HEATING YOUR AQUARIUM

BECAUSE AQUARIUM FISHES ARE USUALLY RE-
ferred to as "tropical" fishes, the idea has become
erroneously established that they require high temperatures for survival. The truth is that 75° F. is warm
enough for tropical fishes, with rare exceptions. In fact,
many of our aquarium inhabitants are only semi-tropicals
and will thrive in even lower temperatures.

Your main concern should be with temperature *extremes*
and temperature *fluctuations*. Too extreme a fluctuation,
even within the favorable range, can lead to difficulty.
Fluctuation even within the fishes' range is the problem
that is usually the most difficult to solve. To illustrate:
most tropicals are comfortable within a low of 70° F. and a
high of 85° F.; 75° F. is considered ideal. But suppose that
the tank's position is near a radiator, or in a sunlit area,
or that the wattage of the reflector bulbs is too high. Any
one of these could cause the temperature to rise to 85° F.
during the daytime. These sources of heat are not present
during the night and the tank's temperature may drop to
70° F. This gives a fluctuation of 15° F. in twenty-four
hours. Fishes continually forced to adjust themselves to
such temperature changes are under a definite strain; they
become weakened and subject to disease.

This does not mean that fishes are extremely delicate.

Considering the abuses to which they are frequently subjected by well-meaning fanciers, they are remarkably hardy. I have seen fishes subjected to such extreme cold that they floated torpid and, to all appearances, lifeless at the surface. When warmed up—and in these cases it was a fairly rapid warming—they recovered promptly and vigorously. Moreover, fishes seem to be capable of swimming without difficulty through strata of water at different temperatures. A reflector might raise the water's surface temperature 5° or 6° higher than the bottom temperature, yet the fishes swim up and down with no sign of discomfort.

There is a school of thought which holds that it is necessary for the temperature to fluctuate a few degrees between day and night in order to more closely duplicate the fishes' natural environment. This hardly seems necessary. Inhabitants of aquariums with controlled temperature fluctuation appear to be in no better condition than those in aquariums maintained at a constant temperature.

That brings us to our first question in our discussion of aquarium heating:

Can't I accustom my tropicals to living in cold water by gradually lowering the temperature?

No. A fish is physiologically suited to living within a certain temperature range. By exercising proper care one can safely bring it to the limit of that range—a limit which varies somewhat with individuals and their condition, as well as with species.

What is the most satisfactory method of heating an aquarium?

An electrically operated heater equipped with a suitable thermostatic control is the most inexpensive and trouble-free method.

What is a thermostatic control?

A control unit employing a bimetallic strip which automatically responds to temperature changes and turns the heater on and off.

How does a thermostat operate?

Aquarium thermostats all utilize the same principle, with variations only in quality, construction and design. The basic principle behind a thermostat is that metal, when heated, expands; and that different metals expand at different rates. Two flat strips of different metals are bonded together. When heated, the metals' unequal coefficients of expansion result in a bending of the strip. One end of this bimetallic strip is fastened rigidly in place and one end of the circuit is fastened to it. The other end is free and rests against a screw in a metal plate to which the other end of the circuit is attached.

As the bimetal strip warms up, it curls away from the screw against which it is resting, thus breaking the contact and the circuit. With the circuit broken, the heater stops heating. As the water surrounding the tube cools, the drop in temperature is transmitted to the bimetal strip, which—being cooled—straightens out again and re-establishes contact and turns on the heater.

How is a thermostat adjusted?

The screw against which the lower end of the thermostat rests is threaded and may be turned to increase or decrease the distance between the points of contact. This varies the extent to which the metal must bend in order to make or break the contact. The metal always expands and contracts the same distance at given temperatures. Once the proper spacing has been reached for the desired temperature setting, it is only necessary to leave the screw setting alone.

The closer the contact points, the more heat is required before the circuit opens. The farther apart, the colder it must get before the contacts come together. In order to raise the aquarium temperature the adjustment screw is turned so as to bring the points closer together, and to lower the temperature, the points should be separated. The diagrams on page 40 illustrate several types of thermostats and the major component parts of their internal structures.

All adjustments should be made gradually and checked frequently with a thermometer to avoid sudden extreme changes of temperature. Usually a quarter turn is sufficient to raise the temperature 3° to 5°.

Some of the more elaborate thermostats have adjustment knobs projecting above the top. They are connected by means of threads or movable plates to the contact points. However, the principle remains the same: varying the distance between the contact points determines the temperature at which the circuit will open and close.

How sensitive is a thermostat?

Some aquarium thermostats are sensitive to as little as ± 1°. However, such extreme sensitivity is not necessary; usually ± 3° is adequate for aquarium use. Some cheap thermostats are even less sensitive and less satisfactory.

What is the extreme range of an aquarium thermostat?

Most thermostats are made to operate at an adjustment between 60° and 110°. Should you try to set the thermostat temperature lower than 60°, the adjusting screw would be at too great a distance from the bimetallic strip, and contact could not be established. Conversely, should you attempt to set the thermostat for more than 110° the screw would be pressed so tightly against the thermostat that the strip could not curl far enough away ever to break contact and stop the flow of electricity.

What is a pilot light?

It is a small light which is hooked into the heater to indicate whether the current is on or off. It remains lighted as long as current is flowing through the heater. The pilot light may be installed inside the tube which holds a combination heater and thermostat; it may be in a separate tube with either the heater or the thermostat; or it may be the plug-in type that fits into the plug, connecting the thermostat and heater. Some combination heater-and-thermostat units have a plastic housing on top, containing the pilot light, condenser, fuse, and connections. In all cases the function and use are the same.

You should make it a habit to check all thermostats regularly. If, in checking, you find that the tank temperature is higher than the thermostat setting and that nevertheless the pilot is still on, you have a strong indication that the thermostat has failed to shut off. It is entirely possible for the tank temperature to be higher than the thermostat setting because the room is warm, or because sunlight is striking the tank. However, when such external factors are causing the temperature rise, the thermostat connection should be open and the pilot light off.

It is also a sign of trouble when the temperature is lower than normal and the pilot light fails to indicate heating. This condition should be checked and corrected. Cheap heater-thermostat combinations can chill or cook your fishes. Check the pages of *Tropical Fish Hobbyist* magazine for nationally advertised heaters; *don't buy substitutes!*

What are the most common causes of heaters failing to shut off?

As the bimetallic strip bends toward and away from contact, an electric arc is created that eventually will pit and corrode the points. To prevent this, a condenser should be attached across the circuit, above the thermostat. Should the condenser short out, the current would by-pass the thermostat, which would then not be operating. The heater, with no control on it, would continue to heat.

Better thermostats today have a fuse in series with the condenser. Should the condenser short out, the fuse "blows." The thermostat and heater, however, continue to function without the condenser and fuse assembly until they can be replaced.

Another cause of trouble is water in the thermostat tube. In this situation the heater continues to function but without any shut-off control.

Occasionally, although not frequently, the silver points that are used today melt and fuse together. This prevents normal opening of the thermostat and is usually a possibility when the power source is direct current (D.C.).

Cleaning the contact points occasionally with very fine sand paper will help correct this trouble.

What are the most common causes of heaters failing to heat?

Usually current failure, or improper contacts in the wall plugs. Occasionally the thermostat plug becomes disconnected without anyone realizing it. All that is necessary to restore its function, of course, is to plug it back in.

Even more infrequent is a burned-out heating coil, or a broken connection within the circuit itself.

Heaters fail to heat only a fraction of the number of times they overheat. It is hoped that the number of times the latter occurs will be lessened considerably by the use of proper fuses.

What is a magnetic snap-action thermostat?

It is a thermostat that operates on the same principle as the ordinary thermostat, but with the following addition. There is a small magnet at the end of the bimetal strip and a corresponding plate on the mounting. As the bending bimetal strip comes close, the magnetic attraction asserts itself, closing the contacts sharply with a snap—hence the name. This rapid closing eliminates the problem of the arc and the necessity for the installation of a radio condenser.

What is a heater?

A heater is the apparatus which provides the actual heat as opposed to the thermostat, which is the automatic switch for controlling heat. The majority of heaters made today are fabricated of nichrome resistance wire, which is wound around a ceramic core. Some are of nichrome which is wound on an asbestos backing, and a few have the resistance element imbedded in the ceramic. The tube may or may not be filled with sand.

Heaters are divided into two groups: those which are attached directly to a thermostat, either in the same tube or an adjoining one, and those called combination units: heaters which are in separate tubes and can therefore be operated as individual units. The first type consists of a heating unit, thermostatic control, condenser and pilot light. For convenience these items may be housed in the same tube with an attached hanger, or they may be located in two different tubes with a clip joining them and a hanger.

At the present time there is only one combination

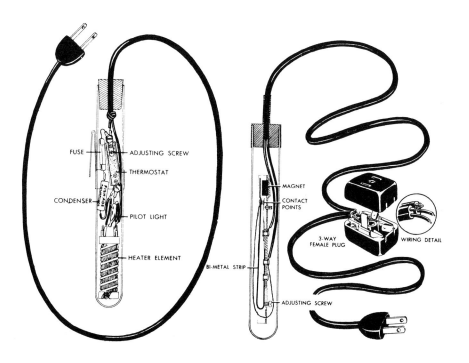

FUSE — ADJUSTING SCREW

— THERMOSTAT

CONDENSER — PILOT LIGHT

— HEATER ELEMENT

MAGNET

CONTACT POINTS

3-WAY FEMALE PLUG

WIRING DETAIL

BI-METAL STRIP

ADJUSTING SCREW

Thermostat and heater combined in one tube.   *Snap-action thermostat.*

heater and thermostat that can be completely submerged in water. Most of them are designed to hang vertically on the aquarium, partly in the water. I specify "in the water" because I have found that a good many people, unless told otherwise, hang such heaters on the outside of the tank.

The water level should be one to two inches below the lip of the tube (or tubes) to prevent water from entering the heater. Always read and follow the manufacturer's instructions carefully.

The cover glass (or hood), if used, should be cut away above the heater and/or thermostat to prevent condensed water from dripping into it.

The combination unit may have a knob on the top to adjust the temperature regulator. This is called an "outside-control." An "inside-control" unit has the mechanism attached to the rubber cork stopper. Removal of the stopper lifts the unit, allowing the adjusting screw to be reached. It is advisable to unplug the unit before it is removed for adjustment.

A word of warning: never put a hot heater into the water; it will crack. Always disconnect a heater before removing it from the water.

The heaters which are made independent of a thermostat may be sealed for submersion or may be hung on the side of the tank. These and the other types mentioned above may be sand-filled.

There are thermostats made which can be used to control one or a number of heaters in several tanks.

What is the advantage of a submergible heater?

A submergible heater is usually placed flat along the bottom of the tank. The theory is that as the warm water rises it will cause a mild circulation within the tank, insuring a more even distribution of heat. Whether this particularly benefits the fish in most home aquaria is doubtful. However, with the heat source at the surface of a tall tank, and with no aeration or filtration, you will note a considerable disparity in temperature between the upper and lower strata of water. Whether the difference, except in an extreme case, is enough to discomfort the fishes is problematical. In nature, fishes swim with no apparent signs of discomfort between the sun-warmed surface and the cooler depths. They appear quite capable of adjusting to this type of change with no noticeable signs of stress.

Most heaters are designed to be attached to the top rim of the aquarium, with only the heating element submerged in the water, but fully submersible heaters (right) also are available.

Why are separate heater and thermostat sometimes recommended?

The theory involving the use of separate units is basically the same as the preceding one. By encasing the heater and thermostat in separate tubes, one is enabled to place the heater in one corner and the thermostat in another. This is supposed to insure a more even distribution of heat, since the heat must travel through the entire tank to reach the thermostat. In theory it is all right, but in actual practice it has hardly proven necessary. Water circulation itself distributes the heat readily enough.

I have a Betta tank which is partitioned into several sections. What type of thermostatic heater should I use and how should it be arranged?

Any type of heater can be used. Judge the wattage required by the capacity of the tank. Place the thermostat and heater in the center section or in adjoining sections. The end sections may be a few degrees cooler than the center, but the difference will not be appreciable.

I have a number of tanks. What is the best way to heat them all?

For the advanced hobbyist who can afford it, the most

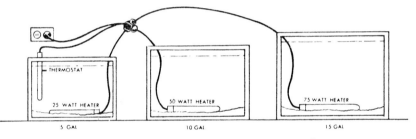

The proper method for heating several tanks using one thermostat.

practical method is a tank room. The temperature in the room can then be thermostatically controlled and heated by the use of a commercial space heater, either gas or electric. A small fan can be used to assure an even distribution of heat within the room.

If this method is impractical, you have your choice of either of two methods, or a combination of both. The simplest way is to get a combination heater and thermostat for each tank. There are a number of low-cost combination units on the market which will give very satisfactory service.

An alternative method is to get a high-capacity individual thermostat. This is placed in the smallest tank of the series to be controlled with the single setup. Heaters with wattages proportionate to the size of the tanks they are put into are connected in series with the thermostat. For the average home, allow 5 watts to the gallon. For a 5-gallon tank, use 25 watts; a 10-gallon tank, 50 watts, and so on.

To illustrate: a hobbyist with four tanks, a 5-gallon, a 10-gallon, and two 20-gallon tanks would use the following: a 25-watt heater in the 5-gallon tank, a 50-watt heater in the 10-gallon, and a 100-watt in each of the 20's. The thermostat to which all the heaters are coupled is placed in the smallest tank. Why? Because the smaller the amount of water in a tank, the more subject it is to fluctuation. Should the thermostat be placed in the largest tank, the smallest one might show a drop of as much as 5 to 6 degrees before the temperature of the large one would drop sufficiently to activate the thermostat.

What are the disadvantages of using one thermostat to control several tanks?

The most obvious disadvantage is that a failure in the thermostat would adversely affect a number of tanks instead of just one. While the well-made thermostat of today seldom fails, it can happen. Another disadvantage is the difficulty encountered in trying to raise the temperature of a particular tank above the norm. Some fanciers keep a small combination thermostat and heater on hand for special uses. When they want to raise the temperature of one of the tanks in the series, they use the combination as an auxiliary. If the tanks are subject to different temperature influences, it would be difficult to control all of them properly from a central thermostat. This might occur when one tank is near a drafty window, or near a radiator whose influence is not felt by the other tanks.

When quite a number of tanks are kept in a room, the usual practice is to arrange them in several rows at varying heights. Unless there is an unusually good circulation of air within the room, the upper rows will be considerably warmer than the lower ones. In such cases it is advisable to use a thermostat for each level.

When there is too great a difference in size between the largest and smallest tanks—say the smallest is a $2\frac{1}{2}$-gallon and the largest a 25-gallon aquarium—it is advisable to use separate thermostats. If there is only one large tank and several small ones, use a combination for the individual tank and a series for the group. If you have a number of small tanks, as well as several large ones, break them up into two groups, according to size, and arrange them in two series.

Is it expensive to run heaters?

No more so than any other small electrical appliance. Remember, heaters are using up electricity only when they are heating. Thermostats do not use up any current; they only conduct it or cut it off.

The warmer you keep your tanks in relation to the room temperature, the more electricity will be required. If you are concerned about the cost of electricity, keep your tanks in the warmest part of the warmest room—but not near a radiator—and maintain your tanks at the lowest safe temperature of 72° to 73° F.

Incidentally, it costs no more to operate a large heater than a small heater in the same size tank. The larger heater will simply heat up that much faster and shut off that much sooner. Many people are under the misconception that a heater gives off only the temperature at which the thermostat is set while heating. This is not so. A heater, once it starts heating, gets as hot as the resistance wire will allow, and stays at that high temperature until the thermostat shuts it off. Then it loses all its heat to the water. A heater does not feel hot to the touch while it is heating, because it is rapidly exchanging its heat with the water. The same heater in air becomes too hot to touch within seconds.

How can I test my heaters?

A test light can be wired to a heater, provided you know how to make the hook-up. If the test light goes on when the thermostat and heater are plugged in, turn the temperature control down until the light just flickers off. If the light fails to go on, turn the temperature control higher. The point at which the light flickers on or off is where the thermostat is set for room temperature. A thermometer in the room will tell you what the room temperature is. From there it is a simple matter to turn the thermostat up or down.

If the light goes on and fails to shut off when the thermostat contact is broken, it is usually evidence of the failure of a condenser, which should be removed. The heater should then function normally. A new condenser should be put on as soon as possible, rather than operating without it. The absence of a condenser puts a strain on the contact points.

If the test light fails to go on, check the male plug and the contact points first; then look for a break in the element, or a black spot, which indicates a burned area.

Occasionally the points become so coated with carbon that they fail to make proper contact, or constant arcing may build up a high spot, preventing the contact from breaking properly. A fine sandpaper used carefully will remove those spots and return the unit to proper operating condition.

How can I be sure that my thermometer is giving the correct reading?

Place your thermometer alternately in warm and cold water to see if it rises and falls properly. Wash the thermometer carefully, and place the bulb edge under your tongue. An accurate thermometer will read close to $98.6°$ F., which is body temperature. A variance of $2°$ or $3°$ is not important, however, since aquarium temperatures are not that critical.

NOTE: *Check a new thermometer for breaks or spaces in the mercury or "spirit" column. These often occur because of jostling during transit. To eliminate such breaks, place the thermometer on a piece of ice until the indicator has retracted completely into the bulb. When the indicator fluid is allowed to warm up, the column should be continuous.*

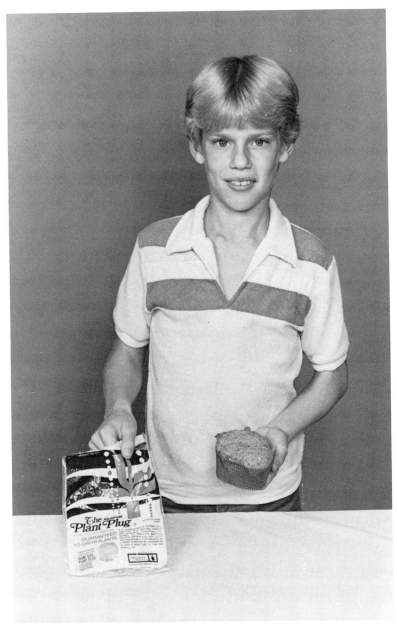

To increase plant growth you can root your plants in nutrient-enriched plant blocks.

CHAPTER IV

AERATION AND FILTRATION

WATER IS THE FISHES' ATMOSPHERE. IT IS THE medium in which they normally exist and through which they travel, and from which they extract the oxygen so necessary to existence. Just as our air must be pure and contain sufficient oxygen, with no excessive amounts of harmful or irritating gases present, so must the fishes' water be clean and well oxygenated.

Provision must be made to prevent the accumulation of harmful materials in the water; whether gaseous, solid, or liquid; whether in solution or suspension. The fishes' water, just as the air we breathe, always contains a certain amount of harmful material; that is, material which would poison the fish if allowed to accumulate above a certain minimal amount.

The atmosphere over every large city contains tons of waste matter such as factory gases and products of combustion. When weather and geographic conditions prevent their dispersal, they can accumulate in such quantity as to inhibit human life. It is this sort of situation which is described as "smog." The same sort of thing, on a lesser scale, can occur in our aquaria unless we guard against it.

The problem is twofold: to insure a proper supply of oxygen for the fishes to use, and to dispose of the products of respiration, metabolism and decomposition.

Oxygen is the fuel that stokes the furnace of life. This is true of fishes as well as of higher forms of life. The majority of fishes breathe by taking water in through the mouth. The mouth is then closed tightly and the water is forced outward over the gills and through openings at the back of the head. Each of the openings is covered by a flap—the operculum—often incorrectly called the "gills." The gills are located under the opercula. They are the red branching members seen when the gill flap is lifted.

A few varieties of fishes, such as the *Bettas* and certain Catfishes, have specialized auxiliary breathing organs which enable them to extract oxygen directly from the atmosphere. However, such fishes are in the minority. It is the gills of the vast majority of fishes that are analogous to our lungs. As the water passes over the blood-rich gill surface, the dissolved oxygen is extracted for the fishes' use, and waste carbon dioxide is given off.

A fishes' nostrils are not used for breathing. The nostrils do not connect with the mouth and are used solely as organs of smell. There are a very few exceptions to this, but they are not included among the fishes kept in home aquaria.

COMPOSITION OF WATER

Each molecule of water is composed of one atom of oxygen to every two atoms of hydrogen. This is expressed chemically as H_2O. Fishes use oxygen, but they cannot use the oxygen that is chemically a part of water. But air, including oxygen, will dissolve in water—just as sugar or salt will—and it is this dissolved oxygen that fishes use.

The major source of usable oxygen in an aquarium is the air above the water. It is therefore at the surface of the water that the major interchange of gases takes place. Carbon dioxide is released by the water at the surface and oxygen is absorbed there. One of the greatest obstacles to an understanding of the maintenance of an aquarium is the mistaken belief that the carbon dioxide (CO_2) and oxygen (O_2) must somehow be in balance. A common belief is that as the supply of one decreases, the other must naturally increase and vice versa. This is simply not true. For example, one can drive *all* the gases out of water simply by boiling it: the warmer the water the smaller the amount of gas it will hold in solution. It is also possible to have an excess of CO_2, enough to cause the death of fishes even though there is an ample supply of oxygen present in the water. It is not enough to supply oxygen to the fishes; a means for disposing of the CO_2 must also be provided.

In practically all natural bodies of water the surface is proportionately many times greater than the depth. In such bodies of water there is also usually a movement of the water caused by wind, current, temperature changes, and so on. These factors assist in the rapid interchange of gases at the surface so that normally water-dwellers do not suffer from a lack of oxygen or an excess of carbon dioxide. In addition, fishes are seldom as crowded in nature as they are in an aquarium.

What is a pump, a filter, an aerator?

A pump is a mechanical apparatus which forces water or air through tubing or other equipment. It provides the flow that makes the filter and aerator operate.

Filters (except undergravel filters) are units containing (or being made of) a porous filter material such as activated charcoal or filter floss. There are a number of different filter types available, but the principle is basically the same in all except undergravel filters. Water from the aquarium is passed through the filter material and thereby cleaned.

An aerator is a unit that exposes water to, or mixes it with, air. As far as home aquaria are concerned, an aerator diffuser is usually a porous stone which is placed in the aquarium with connections so that a pump forces air through it. It serves the purpose of breaking the stream of air into small bubbles, thus increasing its effectiveness.

A water pump draws water from an aquarium through one tube and discharges it through another, the water circulating through the pump. Water pumps are usually employed only in larger indoor installations or in outdoor pools. They may be used to empty aquaria or to transfer water from one aquarium to another. They are also used when it is desirable to have the filter located some distance away from the water to be filtered. Another use, seldom

This vibrator air pump features an adjustable output of air, allowing you to control exactly how much air is released.

encountered indoors, is to spray water for a fountain, or to raise water for a waterfall.

What type of filter and filter material is used with a water pump?

The filter material is the same as that in any other filter, charcoal, and/or sand, and/or glass wool. The filter is designed to be closed tightly when in use, provision being made to remove the filter material for replacement or cleaning. Circulation takes place through two nozzles. The water is sucked through a tube from the tank directly into the filter material. A perforated compartment receives the water after it has filtered through the matrix. A nozzle leading from this compartment directs the water through the pump and back into the aquarium.

This type of water pump usually provides faster and more efficient filtration than do the more conventional types of air-operated filtering systems. However, it does not agitate the water so efficiently as a good air stone; it is also quite cumbersome and usually more expensive to purchase than the ordinary setup.

What types of air pumps are available?

Air pumps are divided into two groups: vibrator pumps and motor-driven cylinder pumps.

What is a vibrator pump?

The same principle of make-and-break current operating in the common doorbell also applies in operating a rubber, leather, or plastic diaphragm which fits over the air chamber of the pump. As the diaphragm moves up and down, air is forced out through one-way valves.

Most diaphragm pumps have a low air pressure but an adequate air volume. They are usually equipped with a knob which controls the volume of air put out. Diaphragm pumps do not usually have so long a life as do cylinder pumps, nor are they so powerful. They are usually less expensive, and for the hobbyist with one or two small-to-medium-sized tanks they are perfectly adequate. They have the advantage of no outside moving parts and do not give off any heat. Nor do they require any oiling or other care. Should they break down, it is usually necessary to return them to the manufacturer for repair. In many cases the guarantee specifies that opening the case voids the guarantee.

Another point of information about vibrator pumps: they must be placed on a firm yet resilient surface, not an unyielding one such as a wall, a table top, or a loose floor board. A sponge rubber pad makes an excellent mounting for a vibrator pump. Such material also helps to eliminate the hum which is an unfortunate feature of some vibrator pumps.

Some diaphragm pumps are very cheap, while others are comparatively expensive. In purchasing pumps, as with other items, you get what you pay for. The lower-priced pumps are not necessarily a better buy. Often they are cheap merchandise offered for sale at a low price. In order to compete, some manufacturers sacrifice quality and reliability so that they can offer a low price. Shop carefully before you purchase a pump, especially if you want it to provide long service. Consider only nationally advertised products.

How does a cylinder pump operate?

A motor is connected by a leather belt to a flywheel. As the flywheel turns, it actuates a piston which forces air out through a cylinder. Some larger models have two cylinders with the flywheel located between them. As one piston enters its cylinder the other is withdrawn, thus providing a continuous flow of air. The amount of air and the air pressure delivered by a cylinder pump are determined by the size of the cylinder, the speed of the motor and the size of the flywheel. The standard motor is from 1/150th to 1/75th horsepower. The volume of air given off by a cylinder pump can, in some models, be regulated by adjusting the angle at which the piston enters the cylinder.

What are the advantages of a cylinder pump?

First of all—power. Cylinder pumps deliver considerably more air and give more pressure than the diaphragm type. They are less subject to breakdowns, and can usually be repaired by the owner with replacement parts, which are available at the pet shop. This eliminates the delay and inconvenience required for sending the pump back to the manufacturer for repair.

What is the wattage consumption of an aquarium pump?

The vibrator pumps consume approximately 2 watts-horsepower of electricity; a 1/150th horsepower motor approximately 29 watts. The cost of running either type, even for twenty-four hours a day, is negligible.

What care does a pump require?

Vibrator pumps require no care; cylinder pumps should be oiled regularly. When purchasing a cylinder pump, always ask for a manufacturer's instruction sheet, which details the proper oiling and adjustment procedures for

This pump and filter starter kit comes complete with a vibrator pump, corner filter, airline tubing, polyester fiber filter and charcoal.

that particular make of pump. Always avoid over-oiling. A drop or two of lubricant is sufficient. Be careful not to drip oil on the electric cord; it will dissolve the rubber insulation. Light household oil is unsatisfactory for oiling pumps, although it may be used for the motor. For the pumps use SAE 30 oil. After a period of service, it is advisable to clean the pump and remove all gummy oil and dirt. The best cleaning agent for this work is carbon tetrachloride. Fill a small oilcan with this fluid, and keep filling the various oil holes while turning the motor by hand. Continue this until the cleaning fluid runs through clean. Allow several hours for the carbon tetrachloride to dry completely both inside and out. Make sure that the motor is reoiled before being put back into use. The cleaning fluid, of course, will have removed all the oil as well as the dirt.

What is the best location for the pump?

It is usually advisable to have the pump at a higher level than the tank. This will prevent any possibility of a siphoning action draining the water from the tank back into the pump. Pump platforms are available for pump placement. These are small plastic or metal shelves designed to hold the pump while hanging on the back of a tank.

If it is desirable to place the pump on the floor, or on any level below the level of the tank, there are several precautions to be observed: Backflow seldom starts while the pump is in operation; it is when the pump is not operating that the greatest danger occurs. Backflow may be started by several actions. (1) The tendency of water to rise in a narrow tube is known as capillary action. If the water in the tank is very close to the top, it is possible for water to rise in the air tube by capillary action to a point where it starts a downward flow and a siphoning action occurs. (2) The cooling down of a warm pump can cause the air inside to contract and draw the water down. (3) Over-oiling the pump can cause excess oil to enter the lines. Air pressure will keep the oil clinging to the inside walls of the vertical tubing, but with the air pressure removed, the oil starts to run back. As it collects in droplets, a vacuum is created behind it strong enough to start a siphoning action.

In order to prevent this, keep a small surgical type "C" clamp handy. When, for any reason, the pump is shut off, clamp shut the line leading to the pump. Also shut all air valves tightly. Whenever oil or moisture is seen in a tube, discard that piece of tubing. It is also a good idea to clean the pump when excess oil appears in the line.

What is an oil and dust filter?

It is a chamber which is cut into the line between the pump and the tank. Its purpose is to catch and hold any oil or impurity that the pump may eject. Usually cotton is used as the oil trap, although occasionally water is the medium used. One commercial trap also has an air gauge attached; thus it serves a double purpose as both an oil trap and a pressure tank. The gauge serves the further function of showing when too much pressure is being built up in the line. By maintaining 2 to 3 pounds of pressure in the pressure tank, a smoother flow of air into the aquarium can be obtained.

How many hours a day should a pump operate?

Aquarium pumps are designed for continuous operation. It is seldom necessary to do this, however. On the average, twelve hours of operation a day, preferably at night, will be sufficient for properly filtering and aerating a tank. Limited operation will also help prolong the life of the pump. In stores and other installations where fishes are crowded beyond the normal capacity of the tank it is, of course, necessary that aeration and filtration be provided twenty four hours a day.

What is the difference between air pressure and air volume?

Air pressure is the force with which air is made to pass out of the pump. Air volume is the actual amount of air delivered. They are both variable and difficult to measure. For our purposes it is sufficient to assess a pump by the number of average-size filters and aerators it can operate in a tank of given size.

Is volume or pressure more important?

A certain minimum amount of each is necessary. An air stone which must operate at a depth of water requires a certain amount of pressure in order for the air to pass through it. The higher the aquarium—which is to say, the deeper under the water the air stone is—the more pressure is required. That is why aquarists frequently find that an

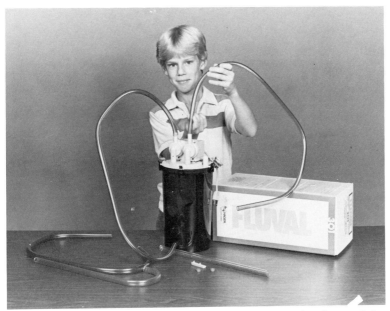

Above: *For larger tanks, biological filters that can be placed several feet away from your aquarium are available.* Below: *Filters that use diatomaceous earth as the filter medium can filter out particles and parasites as small as one micron.*

aerator which emits bubbles when held an inch or two below the surface fails to operate when lowered to the bottom of the tank. The pump simply does not deliver enough pressure to overcome the increased water pressure.

The amount of air delivered is measured as air volume. The average outside filter requires as much air to operate as do five air stones at a 12-inch depth. However, a filter requires far less pressure, because the air is usually required to penetrate only as far as 5 or 6 inches below the surface.

Most vibrator pumps operate with 3 to 6 pounds of pressure. Six pounds of pressure will force a stream of air to the bottom of a 12-foot tank of water. It delivers enough volume to operate 2 filters or 8 to 10 air stones. Small cylinder pumps can deliver as high as 25 pounds of pressure. The volume of air delivered depends on the size and number of cylinders. Smaller pumps will operate 4 to 5 filters, larger ones as many as 12 to 15.

What types of filters are used in aquaria?

Aquarium filters are distinguished by their method of operation. The four types are outside, inside, bottom and under-gravel types.

How does an outside filter operate?

An outside filter is a watertight box suspended outside and alongside of the aquarium. Usually it is made of plastic or glass. The top of the filter is level with the rim of the tank. The filter itself is divided vertically into two unequal compartments by a partition, the lower one-quarter of which is perforated or slotted. The filtering material is placed in the larger compartment. A small tube siphons water from the tank onto the filter material. It sinks through the filter material and runs through the perforations in the partition into the next compartment. The passage of the water through the filter material has cleansed it. The clean water is returned by means of an air-lift tube, which is operated by the pump.

As the intake stem bringing water into the filter is a siphon, it maintains the water in the filter at the same level as the water in the tank. Therefore, the water cannot over-flow. The action is continuous. If the siphoning action is stopped, the return stem—which returns the clear water to the tank—would empty the filter. As the amount of water in the filter is usually small compared to the volume of the tank, no harm is done, that is, the tank will not overflow.

How is siphoning action started?

For an outside filter to operate efficiently, the water level of the aquarium should be quite high, about one inch from the top. The siphon tube is placed upside down in the aquarium to empty it of air. Still held under water, it is righted, and a finger placed over the shorter open end. Holding this tightly closed, the tube is lifted far enough out of the water so that the short end of the stem can be put into the larger filter compartment, the longer end re-maining submerged in the tank. Only now should your finger be removed from the end. The flow should start and continue until the water level in the filter and the tank is the same.

There are several self-starting stems available today. To start them, hold your finger over the opening in the short end and slowly lower the stem into position. Syringe-type starter balls are also available. This type and the automatic or self-starting stems do offer a good deal of convenience.

What is an air-lift or return stem?

These stems operate on the principle that a mixture of air and water in a tube is lighter than water alone and is therefore made to rise by the pressure of the water behind it. The longer the tube, the more effective a given quantity of air will be. The stem is fairly narrow—usually $\frac{1}{4}$ to $\frac{3}{8}$ inch inside diameter. A straight length of $\frac{1}{8}$ inch inside diameter tubing is fastened along the back of the tube from $\frac{1}{2}$ inch of the bottom, and projecting $\frac{1}{2}$ inch above the curve of the tube. The bottom of the narrow tube is sealed shut. A small hole near the lower end permits air to pass from the narrow into the wider tube. When air is forced

Sponge filters are available in many shapes and sizes. These filters trap excess food and waste on and in the sponge. The sponge can be reused indefinitely if it is cleaned periodically.

into the tube, it passes through this narrow entrance and rises in the larger tube, causing the water to flow.

The air flow should be adjusted to give a smooth, even flow of water. If there isn't enough air, not enough water will be raised, resulting in just a little drip. Too much air will cause the tube to spit. Air injected too forcibly into the stem can cause the air to shoot out of the lower end of the tube. The latter most frequently occurs when a powerful piston pump is being used. Frequently a stem's failure to operate is caused by a narrow passageway becoming clogged. Check this by removing the air tubing and substituting yourself for the pump. If you have difficulty blowing through it, the passageway is clogged. Usually tapping the stem smartly on a hard surface several times and then blowing through it will clear the obstruction. I have found that a curved dentist's explorer pick is a great help in reaching this almost inaccessible area.

All air-lift tubes operate on variations of the same principle. The high-speed filter has a hole in the bottom of the clear-water compartment, to which a nipple is affixed. A flexible plastic tube, $2\frac{1}{2}$ to 3 feet long, attaches this nipple to a long air-lift tube. This tube may be anywhere from 18 to 24 inches long. Although this type requires more air pressure than an ordinary 6- to 8-inch stem, by forming a much larger column of air mixed with water, a much greater flow of water results.

What is an inside filter?

Inside filters are usually open plastic boxes with a perforated bottom. A hanger holds them in place on the side or back, inside the aquarium. Only one tube, an air lift, is used. This is fastened to the side of the filter. Water brought up in it drops into the filter, passes through the filtering material and out through the bottom of the filter, directly into the aquarium.

What is a bottom filter?

This is a closed plastic box containing the filtering material. The air-lift tube is straight, instead of curved, and is set in the middle of the filter in the filtering material. This type of filter has perforated sides and rests on the bottom of the aquarium, usually at the rear. The air-lift draws the water from the center. New water comes in through the perforations and passes through the filter material as it makes its way toward the center.

What is an under-gravel filter?

This type of filter uses the gravel bed of the aquarium itself as the filtering material. One type of under-gravel filter is comprised of a sheet of perforated plastic which is placed in the empty aquarium, the gravel being put on top of it. The air-lift tube is located in one corner. It draws water from under the gravel to above the water surface, thus causing water to circulate through the gravel. To date no one has given a suitable explanation for the satisfactory operation of this type of filter. The sludge and dirt seem to melt away and disappear. The effectiveness of this filter is no doubt involved with the action of bacteria, those minute organisms which thrive on decomposing matter. Some bacteria can only live without air; they are called anaerobes. One by-product of their action is hydrogen sulphide (H_2S), a poisonous, foul-smelling gas, the one giving rotten eggs their characteristic odor. Gravel that has decomposing matter in it will soon harbor colonies of anaerobic bacteria. It is probable that the circulation of water through the gravel—induced by the under-gravel filter—destroys the anaerobes and permits the establishment of aerobes which aid in the decomposition of the organic matter without the toxic by-products associated with anaerobes. While this has yet to be proven, it does provide a logical explanation for their effectiveness.

Unfortunately the length of time for which this type of filter is effective is limited. In practice it has been found that the small holes through which the circulation is carried on soon plug up with dirt. For continued usefulness, a bottom filter should be uprooted every six months and cleaned thoroughly.

What is the best type of filter for a beginner?

From the point of view of satisfactory service over a long period of time, an outside filter is the most satisfactory. Hanging in the rear and outside of the aquarium, outside filters are easily concealed yet readily serviceable.

By their very nature, filters become the repository of all the waste and filth in the tank. They should be cleaned every two weeks, on the average, to remove this waste matter. An outside filter is the easiest to disconnect and remove to be cleaned. Also, it can be examined easily to determine the amount of accumulated dirt. If the tank is located where it does not permit the hanging of a filter on the outside, however, it is necessary to employ an inside filter.

A bottom filter is frequently used by dealers for several reasons. It requires a lesser amount of air than do outside ones. Many dealers have their tanks banked closely together, and do not have space between them for outside filters. Also, bottom filters double as aerators. The stream of air agitates the water as it rises, serving to aerate and circulate the fluid.

Against this, however, is the reluctance on the part of a fancier to disturb a tank once it is set up. There is a tendency to let a bottom filter remain without cleaning for months on end, until it becomes a focal point for pollution. Far from serving as a cleansing agent, it becomes a menace. The same holds true of the other types of filters, but to a far lesser degree, because there is much less tendency to neglect them.

Because under-gravel filters have the disadvantage mentioned previously, I usually recommend that they be used in conjunction with a good outside filter. Thus several areas will be served, and there will be less likelihood of difficulty if the under-gravel filter clogs up.

Are homemade filters practical?

In general, it's a waste of time and effort to try to save money by making your own filter.

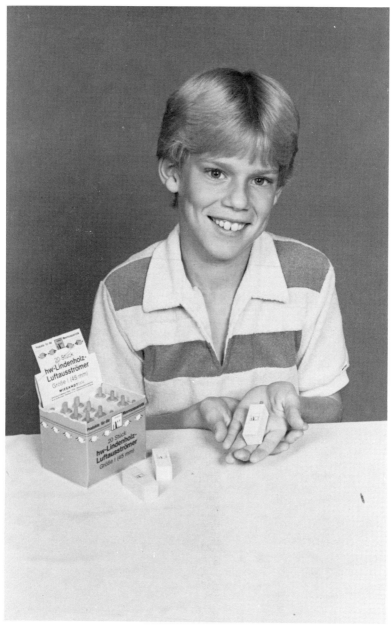

Airstones, such as these wooden blocks, help to circulate the water to release harmful gases and provide fishes with oxygen. They also help to distribute the heat in the tank more evenly.

RED TUXEDO SWORDTAIL
Xiphophorus maculatus

AENEUS CATFISH

Corydoras aeneus

GOLD GUPPY

Lebistes reticulatus

YUCATAN MOLLIES

Mollienisia latipinna

GREEN TUXEDO SWORDTAIL
Xiphophorus helleri

OPALINE GOURAMI

Trichogaster trichopterus

GOLD WAGTAIL PLATY

Xiphophorus maculatus

ROSY BARBS

Puntius conchonius

DISCUS

Symphysodon discus

BLOOD RED PLATY

Xiphophorus maculatus

BUMBLE BEE FISH

Brachygobius xanthozonus

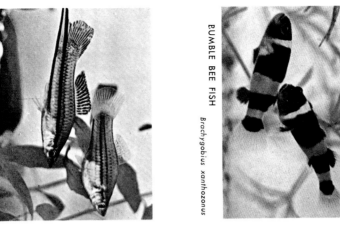

GREEN SWORDTAIL

Xiphophorus helleri

PUNCTATUS CATFISH

Corydoras punctatus

GREEN MOLLY

Mollienisia velifera

REDTAILED PLATY VARIATUS

Xiphophorus variatus

BLUE SPHENOPS MOLLIENISIA
Mollienisia sphenops

MARBLE SAILFIN MOLLIENISIA
Mollienisia latipinna

RED TUXEDO SWORDTAIL
Xiphophorus helleri

DWARF GOURAMI
Colisa lalia

GOLD WAG SWORDTAIL
Xiphophorus helleri

BLACK SWORDTAIL

Xiphophorus helleri

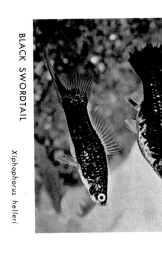

FEMALE BETTA

Betta splendens

COMMON GUPPY

Lebistes reticulatus

WHITE CLOUD

Tanichthys albonubes

MARBLE MOLLY

Mollienisia sphenops

SCHUBERTI (Gold) BARB

Puntius sachsi

FESTIVUM

Cichlasoma festivum

MALE BETTA

Betta splendens

HEAD AND TAIL LIGHTS

Hemigrammus ocellifer

PRISTELLA

Pristella riddlei

FANCY BLUE VEILTAIL GUPPY
Lebistes reticulatus

ALBINO PRISTELLA
Pristella riddlei

PENCIL FISH (Auratus)
Poecilobrycon auratus

BLACK SHARK
Morulius chrysopekadion

GOLD PLATY
Xiphophorus maculatus

CLOWN LOACH

Botia macracantha

KISSING GOURAMI

Helostoma rudolfi

METYNNIS

Metynnis schreitmuelleri

ZEBRA DANIO

Brachydanio rerio

EGYPTIAN MOUTHBREEDER

Haplochromis multicolor

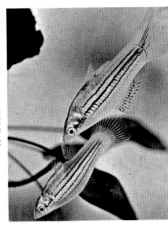

GOLD TUXEDO SWORDTAIL
Xiphophorus helleri

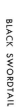

BLACK SWORDTAIL
Xiphophorus helleri

ALBINO SUMATRANUS BARB
Puntius tetrazona

RED WAGTAIL PLATY
Xiphophorus maculatus

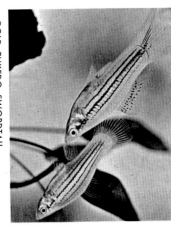

RASBORA
Rasbora heteromorpha

REDTAILED BLACK SHARK

Labeo bicolor

GOLD SWORDTAIL

Xiphophorus helleri

SALT AND PEPPER PLATY

Xiphophorus maculatus

BLUE WAGTAIL PLATY

Xiphophorus maculatus

GOLD WAGTAIL PLATY

Xiphophorus maculatus

SUNSET PLATY

Xiphophorus variatus

GIANT DANIO

Danio malabaricus

NEON TETRA

Hyphessobrycon innesi

ANGELS

Pterophyllum eimekei

RED MINOR SERPAE

Hyphessobrycon serpae minor

BLACK TETRA

Gymnocorymbus ternetzi

REDTAILED SPHENOPS

Mollienisia sphenops

MEEKI

Cichlasoma meeki

SILVER HATCHETS

Carnegiella marthae

ROSACEUS

Hyphessobrycon rosaceus

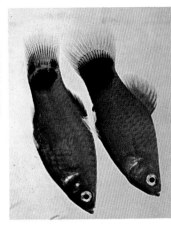

RED CRESCENT PLATY
Xiphophorus maculatus

GOLD CRESCENT PLATY
Xiphophorus maculatus

BRICK RED SWORDTAIL
Xiphophorus helleri

VELVET RED WAGTAIL
Xiphophorus helleri

MARIGOLD PLATY
Xiphophorus variatus

SUMATRANUS BARB

Puntius tetrazona

CARDINAL TETRA

Cheirodon axelrodi

KUHLI LOACH

Acanthophthalmus semicinctus

SAILFIN MOLLY

Mollienisia latipinna

LEERI (Pearl) GOURAMI

Trichogaster leeri

GLASSFISH

Chanda ranga

FANCY REDTAILED GUPPY

Lebistes reticulatus

MARBLE HATCHET FISH

Carnegiella strigata

CHERRY BARB

Puntius titteya

BLOODFINS

Aphyocharax rubropinnis

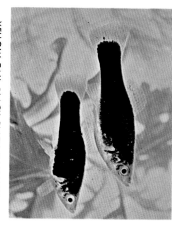

YELLOW TAIL BLACK PLATY VARIATUS
Xiphophorus variatus

BLUE PLATY
Xiphophorus maculatus

BLUE TUXEDO PLATY
Xiphophorus maculatus

PAINTED HYBRID PLATY
X. helleri X X. maculatus

SERPAE TETRA (Common)
Hyphessobrycon serpae

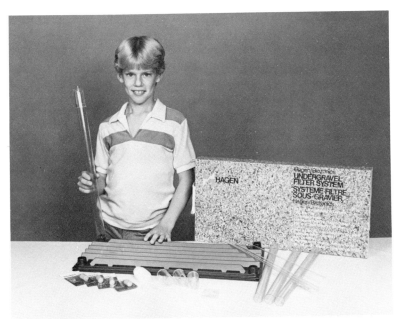

Undergravel filters pull all wastes and excess food through the gravel and store them beneath the plastic plates. In a well balanced aquarium this waste will be broken down biologically.

What is an air release?

This is a small block, usually of porous stone, which serves to break the air passed through it into small bubbles. The quality of the stone is judged by how small a bubble it can produce, while at the same time offering a minimum of resistance to the passage of air.

Reeds are frequently used as aerators. While not particularly efficient, they have the merit of being inexpensive. There are several chrome and stainless-steel aerators on the market today. They use a felt or nylon disc to break up the air. They have an adjustable screw which, by com-

All of the aquarium accessories shown should be purchased together with your first aquarium. After your aquarium is set up you will have to purchase additional equipment for maintaining it.

pressing or releasing the fibrous disc, allows smaller or larger bubbles to escape. There are also a number of so-called ornamental air releases on the market, such as divers, frogs, mermaids, etc. If they are efficient, if you like them and they are not made of toxic materials, by all means get one.

The purposes of aeration are many, for example, to circulate the water gently, thus providing even temperature, and to make filter operation more effective. The prime purpose of aeration, however, is to drive off the carbon dioxide and allow a greater absorption of oxygen. A certain amount of oxygen is absorbed from the bubbles as

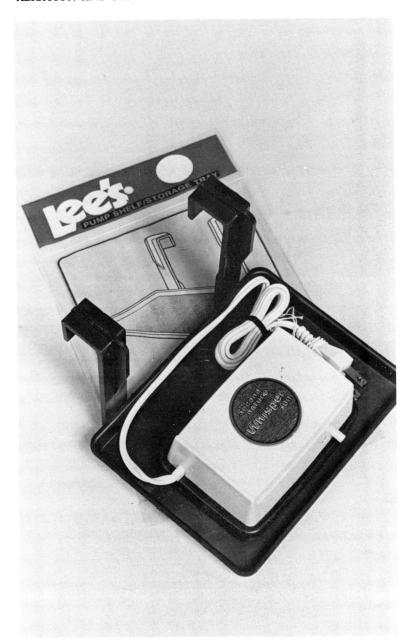

A pump platform is used to keep the pump near the water level so that water doesn't siphon out through the pump—and it's a very handy place to put the pump.

they rise through the water. By far the most effective action takes place at the surface, however. It is the agitation of the surface that gives the best results. As a practical matter, any agitation of the surface will produce the desired results. A small paddle, an electric fan blowing over it, or a drip of water all will aerate the water. A filter also provides a good deal of aeration.

Best results are obtained from a fairly small bubble. A fine, misty bubble does not agitate the water enough. A burst of large bubbles may agitate it too much; also, efficiency is lost with the larger bubbles, since less surface area is being presented to the water for absorption.

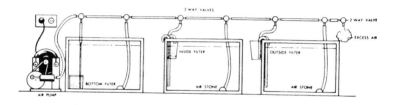

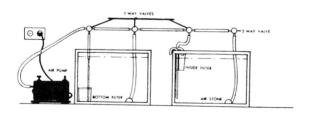

Above: Cylinder pump operating several aquariums.
Below: Diaphragm pump operating two aquariums.

What is the use and the purpose of valves?

Air valves are used to distribute air from the pump through several different outlets. To control the air from a vibrator pump, so that one filter and one aerator may be operated, only one valve is necessary. This must be a three-way valve; that is, one with three outlets or hose connections. The threaded screw controls the opening of the center outlet. The two opposing valves are a by-pass, always remaining open. The square flat tab is usually slipped under the edge of the tank, in back, where the weight of the tank holds it in place. An air tube connects the pump to one of the by-pass outlets. Another piece of flexible plastic tubing connects the center outlet to the air-lift tube, and the aerator is connected to the remaining outlet. The air, of course, takes the path of least resistance. With the valve opened, all the air will pass through the filter, as this offers less resistance to the passage of air. By slowly closing the valve, air will be held back and will seek an outlet through the aerator. Adjust the valve to assure an even flow of air through the aerator. Fishes do not like to live in a storm, so it is good practice to maintain only a gentle flow of air.

To connect a greater number of outlets on one or more tanks, use a three-way valve for each outlet required, a two-way valve at the end. The opposing arms are used to continue the line, with the filter or aerator always connected to the center outlet. Although it is convenient to slip the tab under the base of the tank, it is more practical to fasten the valves to a point above the tank. This eliminates the possibility of water siphoning back through the air line.

CHAPTER V

FURNISHING YOUR AQUARIUM

WITH THE MAJOR EXTERNAL EQUIPMENT PRO-
vided—tank, reflector, cover glass, heating and circulating
equipment—we now turn to the furnishings for the in-
terior of the aquarium.

In practice it is entirely possible to keep fishes indefinitely in a bare aquarium. They do not require gravel,
plants, rocks, or ornaments. But how many people would
keep such an aquarium in a living room? An aquarium to
be properly enjoyed should be a thing of beauty, a
miniature underwater garden.

What is a balanced aquarium?

Originally the concept of a balanced aquarium was that
the standing aquarium is a self-contained microcosm—a
little world. The theory ran that as the plants manufactured
food through the process of photosynthesis, they utilized
carbon dioxide and gave off oxygen. Fishes, on the other
hand, gave off carbon dioxide and utilized oxygen. Fishes'
waste, according to the theory, fertilized the plants, while
excess plant growth provided food for the fishes. One thing
thus balanced another, and no outside care was required.

Unfortunately this theory simply does not hold up in
practice. While plants do give off oxygen in excess of what
they use for respiration, they do so only in the presence of
bright light. When the aquarium is dark, they use up

70

oxygen just as do the fishes. Water cannot store more oxygen than the amount required to keep it in equilibrium with the air above it. Excess oxygen passes off readily. The same does not hold true of carbon dioxide. It tends to stratify, forming layers along the bottom. (Circulation prevents this stratification.) Having a maximum air surface in proportion to the depth thus goes a long way toward keeping the aquarium properly "balanced."

The waste matter produced by the fish is far in excess of the amount required by the plants. Moreover, most of our aquarium fishes are carnivorous, eating animal, not vegetable, matter. Even the more herbivorous species require some animal food.

So the idea of a "balanced aquarium" is a fallacy in its original concept. An "aquarium in balance" is, however, what can be achieved.

What is meant by "an aquarium in balance"?

This is a situation in which all the factors that modify an aquarium more or less balance each other. The proper amount of light (too much overstimulates algae, too little does not permit plant growth); the proper amount of food (too little stunts the fishes, too much pollutes the aquarium); the proper number of fishes; the correct size of aquarium, and the proper temperature, etc. All of these things must be in proper "balance" with respect to themselves and the others if the aquarium is to flourish.

What function does gravel serve?

Gravel is used primarily as a rooting medium for the plants. A depth of 1 to 2 inches is usually sufficient. The greater the depth of the gravel, the greater the likelihood of pollution occurring in it. To avoid pollution, many aquarists put their plants in small pots which are set on the bare floor of the aquarium, even though this does not look so attractive as other plantings. When using this method, it is best to keep a thin layer of gravel, about $\frac{1}{8}$ inch deep, over the aquarium bottom. This will "hold" settlings. It should be siphoned up and replaced with fresh gravel when cleaning the aquarium.

What is the best gravel to use?

Crushed rock, preferably containing no lime, is best. To test for lime, drip some hydrochloric acid on the gravel. If it fizzes, lime is present. A medium grade #2 or #3 gravel is most satisfactory. The size of the granules should be about twice the size of a pin head.

Plants do not grow so well in fine gravel as in coarse; but if the gravel is too coarse, bits of food will drop into the spaces between the particles, where the fishes will not be able to get at them. So gravel size is important. Note: never use sand. Sand is so fine that there is very little circulation throughout. Putrefaction takes place very readily under such circumstances.

What is the best method of washing gravel?

Do not try to wash too much at once: 3 to 6 pounds at a washing is enough. Place this amount in a large pot or bucket. While running faucet water on it, stir the gravel well; then pour off the dirty water. Repeat until no more dirt can be stirred up. Using a sieve or colander for washing gravel is often unsatisfactory. There is then no way of telling whether all the dirt has been washed out.

Should ornamental rocks or other ornaments be used?

Let taste be your guide. Today many aquarium stores feature rocks of all types, as well as glass chunks. Many of these have sharp edges, but there is little reason to believe that the fishes ever cut themselves on them. Mineral or lime-bearing rocks, of course, should be avoided. When in doubt as to the danger of a particular rock or type of rock, test it first, placing it in a tank with a few inexpensive fishes for about two weeks. Rocks serve no particular purpose in the community aquarium (unless it's a community of African cichlids), but many of them are decorative and can be arranged into caves, grottoes, ledges and walls within which or on which some fishes will spawn.

Almost the same could be said of other aquarium ornaments. Bamboo huts, castles, bridges, figurines, frogs, treasure chests, turtles, etc., are available. If you like them and their material and style does no harm, use them to beautify your aquarium.

A word of caution: be sure that all the rocks and ornaments used are set well into the gravel. Do not leave areas under which dirt can drift and accumulate beyond reach. Make sure that such areas do not exist in the ornament itself. And beware of the ornament that has narrow, closed-end passageways. A fish is quite likely to swim up into it and, being unable either to turn or proceed, to die there. Not only will you lose the fish, but its body is likely to be hidden and can pollute the water before being discovered. Many seashells fall into this category. Coral as well as seashells is composed of lime. A small piece or two of coral or a few small shells probably do no harm. In excess, they certainly tend to make the water hard, if it is originally of the soft, slightly acid type. Coral and seashells should be boiled and scrubbed thoroughly with a stiff brush before use.

What is the function of plants in the aquarium?

Although not essential, plants do have a number of uses in the aquarium. Besides being ornamental, they offer refuge to the more timid fishes; they serve as repository for eggs, and a hiding place for babies. They also serve as food for certain types of fishes and breeding places for the micro-organisms on which many fishes feed.

A value which has been attributed to plants is that of reducing or eliminating the growth of algae. The theory has been advanced that the higher plants compete with the more primitive algae for the essentials of life. As far as aquaria are concerned, the case, pro or con, is yet to be proved.

A final and perhaps more general value attributed to plants is that of providing an environment more nearly like the fishes' natural habitat. It is hoped that by more or less duplicating the fishes' natural environment they will thrive more satisfactorily in the artificial confines of the aquarium.

What are the three main groups into which aquarium plants may be divided?

For convenience, plants are divided into groups according to their methods of attachment and growth. These three groups are:

1. **Rooted plants:** Plants with a complex root structure. The growth of new leaves originates at the crown, which is the juncture of roots and leaves. Some plants split at the crown to form two or more separate plants. Amazon Sword Plants (*Echinodorus intermedius* and *E. rangeri*) frequently do this. Others send runners out of the crown. Eel Grass (*Vallisneria spiralis*) is a typical example. A runner is extended along the surface several inches and a new plant is formed there; from this the runner extends to another plant, and so on. Sometimes several dozen are strung out from the original. By cutting the runner, the new plants may be separated from the parent, once the roots of the new plants are firmly established. This will cause no damage to either plant.

Sexual reproduction, which rarely occurs in the aquarium, involves the production of flowers from which the seeds develop.

Any or all of these three methods of reproduction may be used by the rooted group. There are at least two species that utilize two of these methods; that is, flower and root splitting, but instead of runners, the young plants develop directly on the leaves of the parent plant. These two, the Madagascar Dwarf Lily and Watersprite (*Ceratopteris thalictroides*) and Floating Fern, variety of the Watersprite (var. *cornuta*) are called "live-bearing" plants.

In contrast to the next group of plants, roots are essential to many plants of this group. A decaying leaf should be clipped off at the base. In planting, be sure that the crown is at the surface of the gravel, because covering the crown interferes with the growth of the plant. At the end of this

2. **Bunch plants:** These plants take their name from the fact that they are frequently sold in bunches of individual stalks bound together with a rubber band or a strip of lead. In these plants the roots serve primarily as anchors. Growth occurs at the tip. If the tip is broken off, a new one will form; when the stem is injured, a branch often develops. In fact, if the stalk of a bunch plant is thrust into the gravel upside down, a new tip will form at the upper end, and the lower end will develop anchoring roots. The same holds true when a piece of the center section is cut out and planted.

Many bunch plants will grow even while floating freely in water. They show a tendency to root, however, sending down long, thin roots. When these roots reach the gravel, as frequently happens in a shallow aquarium, they anchor firmly and, not infrequently, draw the plant down to the gravel.

The main problem with newly purchased bunch plants is that of anchoring them. They seldom have enough root structure to hold them in place. For this reason it is advisable to plant them in a bunch, retaining the little lead band around them as a weight. Lead is relatively inactive, and a small amount does no harm in the aquarium.

Many bunch plants have a tendency to grow long and shed leaves from the base. The best way to keep this tendency under control is by uprooting the plant, cutting off the lower portion, and rerooting the upper. For bushy, branching growth snip off the tip occasionally.

3. **Floating plants:** These are the plants most frequently used as hiding places for baby fishes. Some of them occasionally put out anchors, called "holdfasts," and these fasten on rocks or submerged bark. Hornwort (*Ceratophyllum demersum*), which is frequently sold as a bunch plant, is really a floating plant. It never develops roots. In others, such as Duckweed (*Lemna minor*), Salvinia (*Salvinia natans*), or Water Hyacinth (*Eichornia*

crassipes), roots are present, but they do not root into anything. They merely float freely below the plant.

Not all floating plants float at the surface. Some, such as Chain of Stars and Stonewort (*Nitella gracilis*), float at the bottom. Reproduction is usually asexual, that is, without flowers.

Is it necessary to use a layer of earth or humus below the gravel?

Some aquarists report good results from the use of a layer of well-washed river mud below the gravel. The dangers of such a procedure far outweigh the possible benefits. Should organic matter be introduced in the mud, its decomposition will pollute the aquarium. The pH of the aquarium is frequently disturbed by the use of mud. Uprooting a plant by the aquarist or natural rooting by a Catfish can disturb the mud and result in a cloudy, messy tank.

Could an excess of plants consume enough oxygen to endanger the fishes?

It is extremely doubtful that healthy growing plants could endanger the fishes in this manner, because they use relatively little oxygen in respiration. However, unhealthy, dying plants are another matter. The decomposition of a plant consumes considerable oxygen and produces quite a bit of waste products. Dead and dying plants are a menace and should be removed.

Can I collect my own plants from lakes and streams?

This is, at best, a doubtful procedure. The chances of introducing fish enemies are great. Plants freshly introduced from the wild state seldom stand much of a chance in the confines and the warmth of the aquarium. Either they grow poorly or die outright. When winter comes, they may stop growing and lose most of their leaves—as they do in nature.

AQUARIUM PLANT CLASSIFICATION

WILLOW MOSS (*Fontinalis gracilis* and *Fontinalis antipyretica*)

A good spawning grass, it is usually found clinging by holdfasts to rocks. Seldom lives long in the aquarium, but it does not decay when dead—retaining its original shape.

WILLOW MOSS

ANACHARIS

ANACHARIS (Water Pest) (*Elodea canadensis*)

Frequently used in Goldfish bowls. Said to discourage the growth of algae in aquaria where it appears. Fast growing and hardy, but prefers a temperature below 75° F.

FOUR-LEAF CLOVER (*Marsilea quadrifolia*)

A good front plant, seldom growing more than 2 inches high.

HORNWORT (*Ceratophyllum demersum*)

A fast-growing plant; growth up to 1 inch a day has been reported. There is a tendency to shed, unless kept under a good light.

FOUR-LEAF CLOVER

FOXTAIL

HORNWORT

FOXTAIL (*Myriophyllum verticillatum*)

Most commonly used for receiving the spawn of egg layers. Unfortunately the fine fronds also catch and hold dirt. This soon gives the plant a messy appearance in the aquarium.

CARDAMINE (*Cardamine lyrata*)

A vinelike appearance makes this plant unusual. Not too hardy.

LUDWIGIA (*Ludwigia alternifolia, L. palustris, L. mulertii*)

There are several closely related varieties of Ludwigia, varying in color from a deep red to a light green. The leaf shape is also variable, ranging from a long narrow to a broad round shape. Undoubtedly light is an important factor in modifying the shape and color of the leaf. Originally a bog plant, Ludwigia takes well to underwater living. A very satisfactory aquarium inhabitant.

CARDAMINE   LUDWIGIA

STONEWORT (*Nitella flexilis*)

Commonly used for shielding the young of live-bearers, its tangled threads are ideal for this purpose. Really an alga, it sometimes fastens itself to rocks. Stonewort grows rapidly in a strong light, but is very sensitive to any salinity.

EEL GRASS (*Vallisneria spiralis*); CORKSCREW (*Vallisneria spiralis* var. *torta*)

These two plants are both reliable standbys. As background plants they are excellent. They are hardy and reproduce freely. Typical rooted plants, they do best when kept in an aquarium by themselves. Alone and under a good light they can be expected to flower. An unfortunate tendency to grow too long can be controlled by clipping the excess growth off the leaves. They are one of the few rooted plants which do not object to this.

CORKSCREW

EEL GRASS

BANANA PLANT

BANANA PLANT (*Nymphoides aquatica*)

Just the tip of the bananas should be placed in the sand. Roots grow from this, anchoring the plant. Quite hardy.

CRYSTALWORT

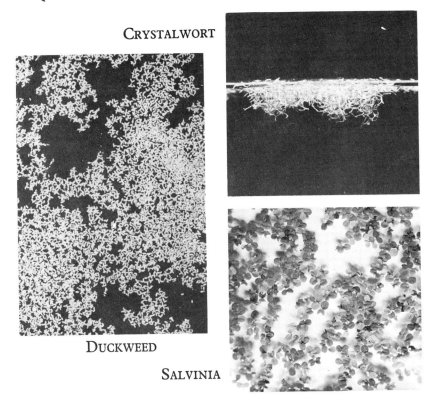

DUCKWEED

SALVINIA

CRYSTALWORT (*Riccia fluitans*)

An excellent hiding place for babies. It should be thinned out regularly to prevent the lower layers from smothering.

SALVINIA (*Salvinia natans*)

Another excellent top cover. It is also useful where the tank is subjected to too much sunlight, providing a satisfactory top shade.

DUCKWEED (*Lemna minor*)

Probably the commonest top grass. Once established in an aquarium, Duckweed multiplies rapidly and must be thinned frequently. It is difficult to get rid of entirely once it has been firmly established.

SAGITTARIA

There are at least seventeen varieties of this plant, from the smallest to the giant *S. gigantea* hort.

Most of them resemble each other, and also *Vallisneria*, closely. They can be distinguished from the latter by the lack of a center rib. They differ from each other primarily in the size and width of the leaf. The *Sagittarias* are heavy-rooted plants and gross feeders. Their roots will help clean the gravel. This can readily be seen when a root grows alongside the glass. The gravel surrounding it will be clean and white by contrast with the rest of the gravel. An excellent all-around plant, it does best when kept in an aquarium by itself. It will compete with *Vallisneria* to the detriment of both if kept in the same aquarium.

SAGITTARIA

HAIRGRASS (*Eleocharis palustris*)

Fairly hardy, it provides excellent bottom cover for baby fishes.

HAIRGRASS

FANWORT

FANWORT (*Cabomba caroliniana*)

Called *Cabomba*, this is the common Goldfish grass. Purchased freely because of its beauty, it seldom holds up well in the warm waters of a tropical aquarium.

AMAZON SWORD PLANT (*Echinodorus intermedius, Echinodorus rangeri*)

The former is a narrower-leafed variety. A truly magnificent plant, the Amazon is the best choice for a centerpiece. Unfortunately it frequently outgrows the small aquarium. Some control over its growth can be maintained by clipping off the larger outside leaves. Another difficulty frequently encountered with this plant is a tendency of the leaves to rot and separate from the crown. This is due to excess dry food dropping into the crown of the plant and should be guarded against. The runners of this plant float above the gravel. As they develop the young plants send down roots which anchor themselves and then draw the young plant down. To remove the shoot without breaking the runner and stopping its growth, hold the runner on the side away from the parent plant in one hand. With the other hand gently work the young plant back toward the parent. It will come loose with surprising ease, and may be planted separately.

AMAZON SWORD PLANT

AMAZON SWORD PLANTS

Cryptocoryne griffithi, Cryptocoryne cordata,
Cryptocoryne willisii, Cryptocoryne nevillii (beckettii)

All of the above make excellent aquarium plants. Heavy-rooted and sturdy, they are very hardy, thriving in a sub-dued light. *C. griffithi* is the plant of choice for a location too poorly lit for other plants to survive. It is also the giant of the group, growing as high as 16 inches. *C. cordata* and *C. willisii* both have reddish-brown leaves differing mainly in that *willisii* has a narrower ripple-edged leaf.

Cryptocoryne willisii

Cryptocoryne nevillii

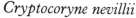

AMBULIA (*Limnophila gratioloides, L. sessiliflora*)

Often mistaken for *Cabomba*, this plant is just as pretty and much hardier. It does not have the distressing habit of shedding.

AMBULIA

SPATTERDOCK

SPATTERDOCK (*Nuphar luteum*)

The rhizome or corklike structure should be planted to the crown. The large bright green leaves make it a good centerpiece. Has a tendency to rest during the winter months.

WATER HYACINTH (*Eichornia crassipes*)

This is not actually an aquarium plant, but a floating pond plant. However, the heavy hairy roots make excellent spawning beds and are frequently used for this purpose.

WATER HYACINTH

MONEYWORT (*Lysimachia nummularia*)

Bright green in color. Not too hardy.

MONEYWORT

Hygrophila polysperma

BACOPA

BACOPA (*Bacopa amplexicaulis*)

A thick fleshy leaf and a minty odor. Fairly hardy.

Hygrophila polysperma

This plant's excellent qualities assure it a permanent place in the aquarium. Hardy, pretty, and fast-growing, it is one of the best of its group. It prefers a temperature above 70° F.

LACE PLANT (*Aponogeton fenestralis*)

A much overrated plant. Valuable for its rarity, oddity, and high price, it is not particularly beautiful. It resembles nothing so much as the skeleton of an Amazon Sword Plant.

LACE PLANT

POOR MAN'S LACE PLANT or CELLOPHANE PLANT (*Aponogeton ulvaceus*)

Far prettier and much cheaper than the Lace Plant.

POOR MAN'S LACE PLANT

WATERSPRITE (*Ceratopteris thalictroides*)
FLOATING FERN (*Ceratopteris thalictroides* var. *cornuta*)

These two plants are treated together because of their similarity, the primary difference being that Watersprite is rooted while the Fern is floating. Uprooted specimens of Watersprite, however, establish themselves with no difficulty as floating plants. A narrow and broad-leafed form of each has been recognized, but it is doubtful whether they are separate varieties or the same plant reacting to different lighting and environmental conditions. Both are so-called live-bearing plants. The young plants appear directly on the leaves of the parents, from which they may be detached to form new plants.

WATERSPRITE

FLOATING FERN

RUFFLED SWORD PLANT (*Aponogeton undulatus*)

A good specimen is a lovely plant. This plant reproduces by flowering or by bulb division, the latter being the more common method. It seems to require a resting period during the winter. Regardless of the fact that the aquarium is maintained at an even temperature all year, the *Aponogeton* will suddenly die down and if not disturbed will make a reappearance several months later.

RUFFLED
SWORD PLANT

MADAGASCAR
DWARF LILY

MADAGASCAR DWARF LILY

A true lily, the Madagascar frequently blooms fragrantly when kept in shallow water—4 to 6 inches. It is quite hardy under most conditions. Its normally brown or spotted coloration gives the impression to those unfamiliar with the plant that it is dying when it is at its best. The lily may divide at the root, or new plants frequently grow out of the leaves.

CHAPTER VII

ACCESSORY EQUIPMENT

MANY OF THE ITEMS COVERED IN THIS CHAPTER are necessary for the proper maintenance of an aquarium. Many of them supplement each other, and many may be constructed at home with very little trouble. Most of the items are to be used for keeping the aquarium clean.

What is a siphon?

A siphon is a tube, made of rubber or plastic, by means of which water can be drawn out of the aquarium into a container which is at a lower level. A convenient size to use is a 5-foot length of $\frac{1}{2}$-inch inside diameter heavy-wall rubber tubing. Heavy-wall tubing is advisable to prevent kinking and collapsing. There are three methods for starting a siphon:

1. Holding the tube to form a U, put one end under the faucet. When water runs out of the other end, indicating that the tube is full of water, cover both openings with your thumbs. Hold one end underwater in the aquarium and the other end in a bucket lower than the aquarium. Release both ends. Once the flow has started, it will continue automatically.

2. Immerse the entire tube in a container of water, keeping the open ends higher than the center so that all the air runs out of it. Place a thumb over each opening, and then proceed as described above.

3. The method most frequently used by experts, because it is fastest, should first be practiced with a container of clear water. It involves placing one end of the siphon tube in the water to be siphoned out. The balance of the tube is allowed to hang down. Suck on the lower end until the flow starts, and then quickly drop it into the bucket. A little practice will enable you to tell by the sudden easing in the resistance of the suction pull that the water has come over the top of the loop and is starting down. It will, however, take a little practice so you won't get a mouthful of water.

An 8- to 10-inch piece of rigid plastic tubing in the end of the siphon hose makes it easier to control and move. The short end in the aquarium is held in the right hand, which guides it over the bottom. The left hand directs the flow into the basin or bucket and regulates the flow, either by pinching the hose or by moving the thumb over the outlet opening.

Stop the flow, hold the suction end about $\frac{1}{2}$ inch over some debris at the bottom of the aquarium, and release the flow momentarily. The debris will be sucked up like magic. By controlling the flow, a maximum of dirt and a minimum of water can be removed. A siphon can be used as a cleansing tool, as a means of emptying the aquarium of water, and as a way of removing gravel—providing the tube is wide enough. In any of these jobs, practice develops control. By putting a funnel at the siphon intake, the siphon will not pick up gravel—only the lighter material. Surprisingly enough, fishes are seldom sucked up in a siphon. Ordinarily, they avoid it when they feel the suction, although when an aquarium is being emptied, fishes that remain as the water is lowered become panicky and will rush up the siphon tube. The rapid trip rarely injures them so long as they land in a container of water and not on a hard surface like the floor.

Lifting the siphon out of the water without closing the ends will empty the tube and break the suction. Should the siphon tube become clogged and resist efforts to blow it out, place it on the floor and walk along it to crush the clogging material.

What is a constant-level siphon?

This siphon is designed to maintain the water level of an aquarium from going higher than a specified height. It does not empty itself when the flow ceases, but remains ready to resume its function automatically when the water level rises. It is especially useful to prevent overflow in aquaria where there is constant inflow of water.

What is a dip tube?

A plastic or glass tube, usually 12 to 18 inches long, comprises the principal part of a dip tube. Glass tubes are extremely fragile, however. There is usually a bulbous section near the bottom, narrowing down again at the mouth. Some models have a flared mouth to eliminate picking up gravel. To operate this tool, one finger is held over the top, tightly closing it. The mouth of the tube is placed in the aquarium directly over the dirt or debris to be removed. When the finger is removed, the water rushes in, carrying the dirt with it. The dip tube is emptied by inverting it into a container. There are also "take-apart" dip tubes which can be dismantled after use for greater ease in cleaning. A dip tube is more convenient than a siphon for removing a small amount of debris and also for working in smaller tanks.

What is a power dip tube?

Actually this unit is a modification of an inside filter operating from the air pump. The air-lift tube is lengthened enough to reach the bottom of the aquarium. Usually a handle is provided for convenience. For best results all the air that the pump provides should be used, the regular filter and aerator being shut off while the power dip tube is being operated.

The power dip tube is held vertically and the intake end moved slowly, just above the gravel. The water picked up in the air lift-tube is passed into the filter, from where

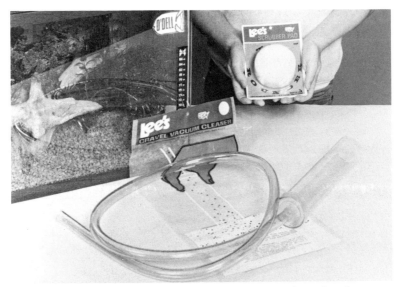

A cleaning pad will come in handy when your aquarium glass becomes overgrown with algae. The gravel cleaner (shown in foreground) is an easy method of removing waste and excess food from your gravel.

it drains through the filtering material back into the tank. Usually only glass wool is used as a filter medium.

The power dip tube is faster than an ordinary dip tube in use, but not so fast as a siphon. It is particularly useful to people who do not have a source of water suitable for fishes readily available and therefore wish to reuse what they have. New aquarium vacuum cleaners serve the same purpose, but have built-in motors and cloth-sack filters.

What is an aquarium scraper?

An aquarium scraper is a long-handled razor blade holder. It is used to scrape the inside of the aquarium glass. Some scrapers have a rubber blade in addition to the razor blade. The rubber is used for removing soft settlings and it is also used like a squeegee to polish the glass. The razor blade is used for the removal of tougher algal growth. This latter type of scraper is not rust-proof and should be taken apart and dried carefully after use. New sponge aquarium glass cleaners are excellent, too.

Should I have a mirror, paint, or "decal" back to my aquarium?

Most tropical fishes are quite thin, and their colors are so delicate that they appear at their prettiest against a background that permits light to enter only from the front and top of the tank. Even when the aquarium is against a wall, light reflection will bounce in. Either a mirror or an aquarium "decal" will provide a decorative background and prevent light from entering the rear. Crystal paint may also be used.

Crystal paint is so called because it tends to crystallize and form patterns as it dries; it is the least expensive background. For best results, the aquarium should be painted while it is empty so that the surface to be covered can be placed horizontally flat. Pour the paint on the back and spread it out with a small brush, pad of absorbent cotton, or even a piece of cardboard used as a sweep. Do not stroke it thin. Only one coat can be applied. The material is fast-drying and usually becomes tacky in an hour or two. However, do not try to rush drying by putting it in the sun or near a fan. Too rapid drying prevents crystallization and the formation of a pattern. If you want to remove the paint, soak several pieces of newspaper with water and stick them to the paint. After soaking five to ten minutes, the paint can easily be scraped off. Crystal paint is available in a variety of colors. A medium shade of green is by far the most popular. New spray cans of crystal paint enable you to apply this beautiful design to a tank already set up.

"Decals" or transfers are available in a diversity of patterns, many of them quite attractive. Mirrors, cut to size and taped against the back of the tank, are very attractive. They give an illusion of greater size. It is impractical to

You will need several types of brushes (shown in center foreground) to clean your airline tubing and filter stems. A siphon or vacuum cleaner will help in removing larger waste particles that collect in your aquarium. Magnetic scrapers are efficient and easy to use for cleaning algae off the glass.

have an aquarium made with a mirror back, however.
There is no particular visual advantage in this, and it is
more expensive. Moreover, when the mirror tarnishes (as
it inevitably will), there is no way of replacing it.

For a tank located in a sunny window, a light background is best. A tank with a light background will remain
10° to 15° cooler than one with a dark background. A
sunshade placed a few inches behind the aquarium is
more effective in deflecting the heat than one that is right
up against the tank.

What are planting tongs?

These are long-handled forceps to make possible the
removal or placement of items in the aquarium without
putting your hands in the water. They are also convenient
for use in closer quarters. In planting, the crown of the
plant is placed in the tip of the tongs with the plant parallel
with the tongs. It is then slid into place. Never poke a plant
straight down. Start an inch or two away from the desired
location and slide it forward and down. If it is placed too
deeply, tug at it very gently and bring it to the desired
height. Two sticks with their ends flattened and notched
are often used for planting. One is used to hold the plant
down, while the other pushes gravel over the roots.

What are planting scissors?

Long-handled scissors which are used to trim aquatic
vegetation. Tying sticks to the handles of an old pair of
scissors works admirably.

What are feed rings?

They are rings, usually glass or plastic, which float.
They are used because dry food placed on the water has
a tendency to spread out over the surface and drop in all
areas of the aquarium. A feed ring prevents this spreading.
Food which drops below it can be located and removed
more easily with a dip tube. Don't get too small a feeding
ring. Make sure that there is room for all the fishes under
it. In some cases one fish will become a bully, driving all

the other fishes away from the ring. In that case, it is advisable to use two or even three rings.

What is a worm feeder?

A worm feeder is made of glass or plastic and is shaped like a cup. It has a number of small perforations in the bottom. It floats at the surface. *Tubifex* or white worms, when placed in it, wriggle slowly through the holes, to be consumed by the waiting fishes below. This eliminates the possibility of their crawling into the gravel, as might happen if the worms were just dropped into the water. It also enables you to determine just how many worms the fishes eat. As with the feeding ring, so with the worm ring: if you are feeding a large number of fishes, or if one fish dominates the feeding area, use several rings.

There are different types of worm feeders available.

A worm feeder will keep live tubifex worms in one place. This will allow all of your fishes an opportunity to feed on the worms and prevent the worms from entrenching themselves in the gravel.

What are breeding traps?

They are plastic containers. There are three types: the rod trap, the "V" bottom, and the combination nursery and breeding trap. They are all designed to hang inside an aquarium and receive heat from it. They are also perforated to allow water circulation. Very little actual circulation takes place, however, unless it is helped along by dipping water out of the tank proper and pouring it gently into the breeding trap. The excess will, of course, run out through the perforations. Usually a breeding trap is set in the rear of the aquarium where its inhabitant will not be disturbed.

The **rod trap** is a square box about 8 inches long by 4 inches wide by 4 inches high. The bottom consists of glass or plastic rods set a little apart from each other. The pregnant female is confined in this type trap with a few sprays of plants for hiding herself. This is important, because in a bare trap there is more of a tendency for her to thrash around. When the young are born, they drop through the bottom and are protected from the possible cannibalism of their mother. Of course there should be no fishes in the aquarium into which the babies drop.

This same type of trap, but longer (up to 18 inches), is also used for breeding certain egg-laying fishes, such as Zebras (*Brachydanio rerio*) and White Clouds (*Tanichthys albonubes*), which lay non-adhesive eggs. The egg-hungry fishes breed in the trap and the eggs drop through out of reach.

The **"V" bottom trap** is shaped so that the bottom comes to a long V. The sides are perforated. Babies, when born, drop out through the slit. This type is also provided with a plastic rod or strip which can be used to close the bottom and prevent the babies escaping. This is used when there are fishes in the larger aquarium which might eat the babies. Of course they are still in danger of being eaten by the mother, but putting some hiding plants (see Chapter V) in the trap will help save at least some of them. Do not overdo the hiding plants, however; leave room for the mother.

The **combination breeding and nursery trap** is a square box with a "V" insert in it. When born the babies drop through the opening in the bottom of the vee and are confined in the lower portion of the trap. After delivery, the mother and the insert are removed, giving the young ones a nursery to swim around in. As might be expected, this type is somewhat more expensive.

Since all of these breeding traps are comparatively small, it is inadvisable to keep large females in them. They will suffer from the confinement. And of course never keep two females in the one trap. Cover breeding traps, because even baby fishes can jump.

A trap is not so satisfactory a method of raising babies as a separate nursery tank is. It is, however, of great value to the person who cannot keep more than one tank and still wants the thrill of breeding his own fishes. A breeding trap may also be used in conjunction with a baby tank. Obviously you cannot keep an adult gravid female with the babies while she is awaiting delivery. A breeding trap is placed in the baby tank and her babies join the others as they are born.

Whether in a trap or a tank, babies must be fed. To accomplish this, use special baby foods. Feed small amounts, but feed frequently. Do not give the little stomachs a chance to get empty. Do not make the meals too big, as the excess will spoil before the babies have had time to eat it.

What are suction cups used for?

These are small rubber suction cups with a rubber band or a thin stainless steel wire attached. They have many uses in keeping the aquarium neat. They can be used to keep air-line tubing in place, to keep feed rings from floating away, to attach thermometers in an easy-to-read position, and so on.

What is the best type of net?

A square nylon mesh net of a size suitable to the aquarium is best. It is much easier to catch fish with a large net than with a small one. Too often people try to catch an active fish with a soupspoon-size net. They simply end up with frayed nerves, torn plants, and an exhausted fish. Small nets are useful for driving the fishes out of the plants into the large net, which does the actual catching.

What is chlorine neutralizer?

Many municipalities add chlorine to their water supply as a disinfectant. Chlorine in sufficient quantities will kill fishes. Chlorine is a gas that will dissipate itself from water which stands exposed to air for a few days. The liberation of chlorine can be hastened by aerating or by splashing the water. Products known by various trade names can be used to "neutralize" the chlorine. These are available in crystals, tablets, or liquid form. They are all equally effective. The liquid form is by far the most convenient to use.

The purpose of using a chlorine neutralizer is to make the tap water suitable for fishes' use without waiting for the water to age and to lose its chlorine. Several complex chemical changes take place in the water during this aging process in addition to the liberation of chlorine. These changes tend to make the aged water more suitable for fishes than the raw tap water is.

Fishes prefer the aged water, but if for some reason you cannot take the time to age it, then by all means use the chlorine neutralizer. Water should be aged in glass, enamel, or stone containers. Never use metal containers.

What is a pH testing kit?

pH is a measure of the acidity or alkalinity of the aquarium. This value is expressed in numbers: 7.0 is neutral; a value above 7.0 (7.4, 8.0, etc.) is alkaline; below 7.0 is acid (6.9, 5.8, etc.).

The majority of our aquarium fishes thrive at a pH near neutral. Most fishes will withstand a change from water of one pH to water of another pH provided the change is gradual.

There are two types of inexpensive kits available to

Plastic rocks can be pieced together and used to form rock caves and walls useful in aquascaping.

Ceramic ornaments are available in hundreds of realistically molded forms. These ornaments are safe for your fish and easy to keep clean.

aquarists for measuring pH. One involves the use of a liquid indicator dye, bromthymol blue. A drop or two of the indicator is placed into a measured amount of aquarium water. The color of the sample is then compared with a color chart provided for that purpose.

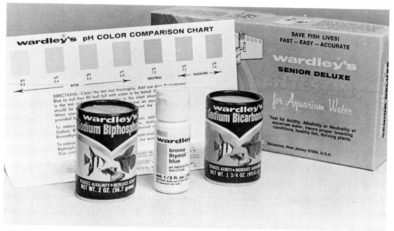

Testing your water is an important part of maintaining a successful aquarium. This kit allows you to keep a constant check on the pH level of your water and comes complete with the necessary chemicals for adjusting your water as well.

Also useful is the roll of impregnated paper which is specially designed for accurate pH readings. It contains a roll of paper in a plastic dispenser. A small strip of this paper is torn off, dipped into the water, and held up a few seconds to dry. The drop of color which forms on the end is then compared with the color chart which is provided on the case of the pH tester.

pH can be altered by the addition of chemicals: sodium bicarbonate to make it more alkaline, and sodium biphosphate to make it acid.

A properly set up and cared-for tank will remain at or

near neutral by itself. A constant variation or tendency to become too acid or alkaline indicates an unbalanced tank and should be investigated.

What is a water hardness testing kit?

This is a kit containing ingredients for measuring the amount or number of grains per gallon of the dissolved salts of magnesium or calcium present in the water.

There are two types of kits available. The first involves the use of three chemicals which are added in succession to a sample of water to be tested. The number of drops of the last solution required to change the color is a measure of grains of hardness per gallon. The second type of kit makes use of the fact that soap will not lather readily in hard water. Drops of a standard soap solution are added to a sample of water. The number of drops required to produce a lather equals its hardness in grains per gallon.

A rough idea of the hardness can be gained by washing your hands in some of it. Soft water lathers readily.

Like pH, there is a good deal of controversy as to the practical importance of water hardness. Most fishes can certainly stand extremely hard water if they are gradually accustomed to it. Many fishes will breed much more readily in soft, slightly acid water. There are chemical water softeners which will remove the calcium and magnesium salts from water. There are also water demineralizers available. These remove all the dissolved minerals from the water, leaving it almost as pure as distilled water.

Neither of these should be used on water while the fishes are present. Fishes cannot live in distilled water. To avoid overdoing it, when your water is too hard, make changes carefully. Soften some water separately. Dilute your aquarium water by adding this water to it and testing frequently. The amount to add depends on the degree of hardness you start with and the degree of hardness required. A hardness of 3 to 9 grains of hardness is the most satisfactory, although as stated before most fishes can stand water much harder than this, if the change to it is gradual.

Hardness is frequently measured as parts per million, abbreviated as p.p.m. Divide the number of parts per million by 17.1 to find the grains per gallon.

CHAPTER VIII

SETTING UP YOUR AQUARIUM

SETTING UP THE AQUARIUM INVOLVES THE WORK of assembling the component parts, whose construction and uses we have discussed in the preceding chapters. Although the sequence of the preceding chapters may seem to be inverted, the purpose of this book is to make the setting up of your aquarium as simple as possible. Knowing all the parts involved, you will now have a better understanding of the whole.

To make it easier, there will be references here to data in preceding chapters so that you can refresh your memory on those points.

Setting up an aquarium is a process which can be systematized to save effort. If you follow the sequence of suggested operations given below, you will save yourself a lot of time, trouble, and work.

PREPARATION: Wash your hands well and rinse them very thoroughly. It is not dangerous to put your hands in the aquarium even after the fishes have been put in, but it is only reasonable to have them clean to avoid the possibility of introducing toxic materials. Wash the tank thoroughly, using rock salt on a clean rag in place of scouring soap. Never use soap or any detergent to clean the inside of an aquarium. While they are not as dangerous as most people believe them to be, sufficient soap residue might very well cause trouble for your fishes. The little salt which might remain after the tank has been rinsed several times will do no harm.

APPLY BACKGROUND: If a "decal" or paint is to be used, now is the time to apply it while the tank is empty and easy to move. (See page 96.) Positioning a mirror can be postponed until after the planting has been completed. Be sure that the background paint is dry before standing the tank upright.

TANK PLACEMENT: Set the tank in what is to be its permanent position or location. Once the tank is filled, it is difficult to move without causing leaks. If moving the tank is necessary, siphon out at least three quarters of the water first. (See page 92.) Make certain that the tank support is strong enough to hold it, and be sure that the surface is level.

PUT IN THE GRAVEL: Well washed gravel should now be spread out in the tank. It should slope from a high point along the back and sides to a lower area at front and center. The under-gravel filter, if one is to be used, must be placed on the bottom of the tank before the gravel is added, of course. In placing the gravel, a depth of 2½ to 3 inches along the back and sides, sloping to 1 to 1½ inches along the front, is satisfactory. If an under-gravel filter is used, follow the manufacturer's directions about the depth of gravel to be placed above the filter.

SET IN ROCKS, ORNAMENTS, ETC.: Now set in the objects you have chosen for your underwater scene. (See page 72.) If a diver or other ornamental aerator is to be used, attach the tubing to it before putting it into the tank. See that no crevices are left for dirt to drift into. Draw an imaginary line along the bottom from the center rear to each front corner. All rocks and ornaments, and, later, the plants, should be set behind the two lines, larger items in the rear, smaller ones toward the front. This makes a pleasing arrangement, assures an even lighting for the plants, and allows for a clearing in front so the fishes may easily be seen.

COVER WITH PAPER: A sheet of brown paper, or wax paper, or several layers of newspaper are now placed over the gravel. Stand a saucer or cup on this, and pour the water gently into the cup or saucer.

It is best to use water of about 75° F. for filling. Where the water is too cold, heat some and mix it with the cold water. This should be done in a separate container before putting it into the tank. Adding hot water to the tank

Neon Tetras in a prize-winning home aquarium.

can crack it. Usually running some hot water from the tap as the cold is drawn is the most satisfactory method of tempering the water.

For a large tank (more than 20 gallons) it is best to fill it only half full and postpone the balance of the work for a few days to allow the cement to settle. Smaller tanks may be filled to within a few inches of the top. The cup or saucer is then removed, and the paper drawn out by the edges. Do not wring the paper out in the tank.

Straighten out any pockets in the gravel caused by the filling; rearrange any rocks that may have moved.

If you have followed these instructions, the water will be reasonably clear and easily seen through. If it is gray or muddy, the gravel was probably not washed well enough. It will settle out if it stands, but any disturbance of the gravel will roil it up again. Under these circumstances it is best to empty the tank with a siphon and rewash the gravel.

FILTER, AERATOR, AND HEATER: Hang the filter in place (see page 58), and put the stems and aerator into position. Do not attempt to start it yet. Hang the heater and thermostat in place (see page 36), but do not plug them in.

PLANTING: Plant the larger plants in the corners first. One large, bushy plant, such as the Amazon Sword Plant, or a *Cryptocoryne* may be used as a center plant at the apex of the imaginary triangle. The rest of the plants in order of size are gradually placed in the sides, working from front to back.

Trim off any dead leaves and rinse the plants well before putting them into the tank. A good light on the tank while working makes planting work easier.

To plant, use planting tongs (see page 98), or hold the plant an inch above the crown, between the tips of the thumb and the middle finger. With your hand held fingers down and the roots pointing down, the body of the plant now extends into the palm of your hand. Place the ball of your index finger on the crown of the plant. Then place the plant on the gravel a few inches away from the desired location. Slide the plant forward and down into the gravel so that it ends up in place. Should it be rooted too deeply, tug it up gently. Exceptionally long roots may be trimmed down to 2 or 3 inches. If you do not care to cut them, then gather them up into a more compact mass for ease in handling and planting.

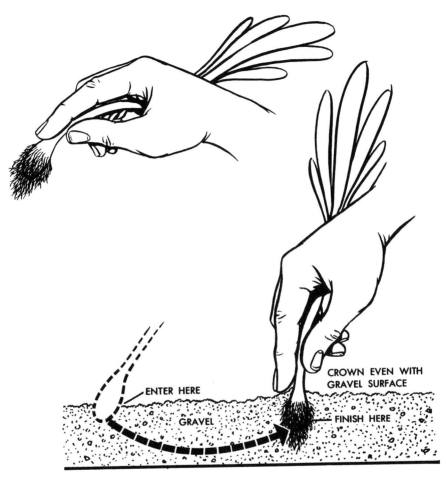

Proper method of planting.

Some particularly buoyant plants, such as *Sagittaria* and Watersprite, should be left planted deeply for three or four days. When the roots have had a chance to spread out a little, the plant can be pulled into position.

FINISH FILLING: Hold your left hand, palm up, just under the surface of the water. Hold the pitcher or bucket in the right hand and gently pour water into the left hand until the aquarium has been filled to a point just above the lower edge of the frame. A tank looks prettier when the waterline does not show.

Start the filter going, and plug in the heater. Be sure that the thermostat is set properly.

If you must put the fishes right in, add chlorine neutralizer to the water. Check the pH, which has not had time to adjust itself. If necessary, adjust it to neutral (see page 102). If you are going to wait a few days before putting the fishes in, do not check the pH until then. The chances are that the pH will adjust itself, given a little time.

Many fanciers advocate the addition of 1 teaspoonful of coarse salt to each 5 gallons of aquarium water when setting up a tank. This need not be repeated, unless water is drawn off and replaced when the same proportion of salt is replaced with it. The reason is that salt does not evaporate, but remains permanently in the aquarium.

Within a few hours after filling, tanks filled from the tap will have bubbles formed on the glass. These are excess gases which were dissolved in the cold water. The same gases may be seen forming bubbles when water is heated on the stove. These bubbles may cover everything, including the fishes. They are frequently mistaken for signs of disease on the fishes. The bubbles will disappear permanently within forty-eight hours.

EXTRA LIGHT: The reflector should be allowed to burn steadily for the next seventy-two hours. This will help give the plants a good start.

RECEIVING FISH SHIPMENTS: Many people receive fishes shipped from out-of-town sources. Often prompt and proper action must be taken upon their arrival to insure their continued life.

Examine the carton carefully before opening it. If it is wet or damaged, mark the fact on the receipt before signing it. Make the carrier wait and watch while you open the shipment. Check the water temperature immediately. Do not remove any fishes which appear to be dead, unless they are obviously decayed or physically damaged. Many torpid fish can be revived.

If the water is below 70° F., it is important to warm it to a higher temperature. Do not remove the fishes and put them into other warmer water. Instead, add warm water to the original water. Stir as you add the warm water to prevent hot water from touching the fishes. Warming the water slowly is dangerous. The fishes may die before the water gets warm enough to help them.

Aerate the water. Once a desired temperature has been reached, change part of the water for fresh water. If the original water was foul, continue making partial changes at intervals until the water is clear. The water which is dipped out is thrown away. This process over a period of hours will give the fishes a chance to adjust to the different composition of your water.

INTRODUCING FISHES INTO THE TANK: Fishes are usually brought home in a small container from some local source. These containers should be allowed to float unopened in the aquarium for fifteen minutes. This allows the water in the container to equal the temperature of the tank water. Remove the cover carefully. The fishes are likely to jump as soon as they see the light. Partially submerge the container slowly so that some water from the tank gradually runs into it. Pour out part of the water and repeat. Do this several times before completely submerging the container and letting the fishes swim out.

When transferring fishes from one tank to another, the same procedure is followed. Dip some of the fishes' own water out in a container and place the fishes in that for transferring. It is unnecessary to float the container first, however, if the two tanks are at the same temperature.

Be careful in introducing new fishes into inhabited tanks, particularly when the newcomers are smaller than the occupants. When doing this, it is best to feed the fishes in the front, and while they are busy eating, quietly introduce the newcomers in the back.

QUARANTINE TANKS: Many aquarists maintain newly acquired fishes in separate tanks for ten days or two weeks. This helps to reveal any latent disease before it might be transmitted to the other fishes. During this time strict isolation is practiced. Utensils (net, dip tube, etc.) are disinfected, water drips are avoided, and even hands are scrubbed and rinsed thoroughly before going from one tank to the other.

A fairly good isolation ward for two or three small fishes is a squat one-gallon jar floating in the aquarium. By experimenting with the amount of water in the jar, you can determine the proper amount to keep it upright and buoyant. This type of jar can be used for breeding also. A breeding trap, with its perforations which permit the circulation of water, is of course valueless for isolation.

FEEDING: Do not feed the fishes for a day after their arrival. They are usually too disturbed to eat, and if the food is not eaten it decomposes and pollutes the water.

After twenty-four hours, feed sparingly once a day. When the fishes have settled down and are eating regularly, start twice-a-day feedings. Always feed sparingly, no more dry food than can be consumed off the surface of the water in one and one-half to two minutes. Always leave the fishes hungry enough to search over the bottom for any food that may have dropped from the top. The average fish's stomach is the size of its eye. It can eat at one meal only about as much food as would cover one eye.

Very few fishes can eat in the dark. Never feed just before turning the lights off or immediately after turning them on. In the first case, the fishes need time to pick

Properly treated driftwood makes an attractive addition to the aquascaping of your aquarium. Wood that is not properly treated will slowly kill your fish, as it reacts with your aquarium water.

all the food off the bottom; in the latter case, it takes fishes ten or fifteen minutes to adjust to the light after having been in the dark for some time. By the time they have adjusted sufficiently to eat, the food will all have sunk to the bottom.

Signs of overfeeding are recognized as cotton puffs on

the bottom and plants, as a gray slime over the bottom, as milky water, and as black gravel. As the particles of food are smaller than the granules of gravel, uneaten food works down into the gravel until it reaches the slate. It lies there and rots, and as more and more waste food works down, the putrefaction spreads up toward the surface of the gravel.

People are frequently surprised when they stir up the gravel in their tanks and reveal what has been festering below an apparently clean surface. A light, occasional stirring of the gravel will help prevent this situation from developing. Best of all, prevent it by not overfeeding.

HOW MANY FISH: There are many formulas available to compute the number of fishes that a given quantity of water will support. Unfortunately, because of the many variable factors, none of the formulas is very dependable. The old, simple formula, which is still in use, is as good as any of the more complicated ones: as a maximum, allow one inch of fish, exclusive of tail, per gallon of water. Double this if a filtering system is in use. The average-sized tropical fish is 1 inch.

Bear in mind that if you crowd your tank up to the maximum permitted with a filtering system, you become dependent on artificial aeration. Should this break down, you will probably have difficulties on your hands.

I personally feel that it is much more advisable to stay well below the limits imposed by the above formula. I find that although fishes live at those limits they thrive better, grow better, and remain healthier when less crowded.

At any rate, start off with about half the amount of fishes recommended by the formula. Then gradually add to your collection. Add a few fishes at a time to allow for adjustments. A well-set-up and properly cared-for aquarium can support much more than this original amount, so by using the formula and observing its limits you will be quite safe.

CHAPTER IX

TYPES OF AQUARIUM FISHES

THE FOLLOWING IS A LIST OF AQUARIUM FISHES with their outstanding characteristics. Some of these are subject to individual interpretation. For example, individuals of most species listed as pugnacious may be safely kept with other fishes while still small. Also, the young of certain fishes which grow to a large size may be kept in smaller aquaria than indicated on the chart.

Certain fishes may be harmless to other fishes, but should not be kept with fishes of their own species. The outstanding example of this is the Siamese Fighting Fish. It is listed as a community fish, but an adult male *Betta* should not be kept with another *Betta* of either sex, except with a female while breeding.

Certain fishes have a tendency to school. In some this instinct is so strongly developed that they are actually upset if they aren't kept in the company of their own kind. Many fishes that ordinarily school may swim by themselves in a tank of mixed fishes, and fishes that do not ordinarily school together may, under the pressure of certain circumstances (of fear, etc.), form a school for a limited period of time.

Fishes that seldom school are indicated by an ★ mark in the chart. Those fishes that prefer the company of several of their own kind are so indicated by an ★★ mark. Those fishes that are unhappy unless in a school have an ★★★ mark in the chart.

Under the title of community fish in the chart, a single ★ mark indicates those fishes that should be kept only with other fishes their own size or larger. The mark ★★ indicates suitability for a mixed tank but a tendency to fight with others of their own species.

Certain fishes cannot readily be kept in the average community tank. This may be due to particular feeding requirements, a necessity for special water conditions or

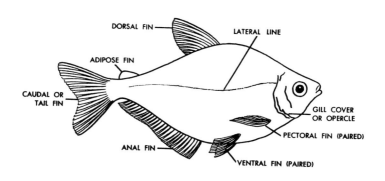

some other requirement which is not easily satisfied. These fishes are indicated on the chart with a mark of ★★★. It is suggested that more knowledge of these fishes be acquired before they are purchased.

Fishes that are good all-around community fishes, hardy, easily fed, and fairly peaceful are marked ★★★★. Of course one must consider individual variations within a species. For instance, although Guppies are considered ideal aquarium fishes, I once owned a male Guppy that had a positive penchant for killing Neons. He ignored other small fishes, but pursued Neons vigorously and would kill any placed in a tank with him. There are very few fishes that do not consider a small "bite-sized" fish a suitable meal.

Such facts must be borne in mind in working from the list of fishes considered suitable for a community tank. Within reason, the fishes in the chart under the "Community Fish" heading having a mark of ★★★★ can be mixed with each other. The important thing to remember is to keep the extremes in sizes separated.

Under the heading of "Size of Adults" in the chart, one ★ indicates that the individual fish cannot be expected to reach 3 inches in length. A mark of ★★ indicates 3 to 6 inches at maturity, and a mark of ★★★ indicates a fish that can be expected to reach a size greater than 6 inches in length under suitable conditions. All of the fish measurements given exclude the tail.

Under the heading "Size Tank Required" one ★ indicates that the adult of the species will live in a tank of 5 gallons or less capacity. The mark ★★ indicates a requirement of 5 to 15 gallons; and a mark of ★★★ indicates a larger tank than 15 gallons is required. Of course fishes that will live in the smaller tanks will be quite happy in the larger ones.

Under the heading "Breeding Habits" one ★ indicates a live-bearer which spawns readily. An ★★ indicates an egg layer which has frequently been bred. A mark of ★★★ indicates an egg layer that is seldom or never bred in captivity. I am placing Neon Tetras (*H. innesi*) and Red Rasbora (*R. heteromorpha*) in the second category. While not spawning as readily as we would wish them to, they have now been bred too frequently in captivity for their spawning to be considered a rare occurrence.

Fishes are listed alphabetically by their scientific names. The common names are given also. This was done to avoid confusion. Common names may vary both locally and nationally, but the correct scientific name is always the same.

	Tendency to School	Community Fish	Required Tank Size	Breeding Habits	Size of Adults
Abramites microcephalus Striped Head-stander	★	★★	★★	★★★	★★
Acanthophthalmus semicinctus Kuhli Loch	★	★★★	★	★★★	★
Aequidens latifrons Blue Acara	★	★	★★★	★★	★★★
Aequidens maronii Keyhole Cichlid	★	★★★★	★★	★★	★★
Aequidens portalegrensis Port Acara	★	★	★★★	★★	★★★
Ambassis lala Glass Fish	★★	★★★★	★	★★	★
Anabas testudineus Climbing Perch	★	★	★	★★	★★★
Anopticthys jordani Blind Cave Fish	★	★	★	★★	★★
Anostomus anostomus	★	★★	★★★	★★★	★★★
Aphyocharax rubripinnis Blood Fin	★★	★★★★	★	★★	★
Aphyosemion australe Lyre Tail Panchax	★	★★★	★	★★	★
Aphyosemion bivittatum	★	★★★	★	★★	★
Aphyosemion coeruleum Blue Gularis	★	★★★	★★	★★	★★
Aphyosemion gulare Yellow Gularis	★	★★★	★★	★★★	★★
Aphyosemion sjoestedti	★	★★★	★★	★★	★★
Apistogramma agassizi	★	★★★★	★	★★	★★
Apistogramma ramirezi	★	★★★★	★	★★	★

	Tendency to School	Community Fish	Required Tank Size	Breeding Habits	Size of Adults
Aplocheilichthys macrophthalmus Lamp Eyes	★★	★★★★	★	★★	★
Aplocheilus lineatus Panchax lineatus	★	★	★★	★★	★★
Astronotus ocellatus "Oscar"	★	★	★★★	★★	★★★
Badis badis Chameleon Fish	★	★★★★	★	★★	★
Barbus conchonius Rosy Barb	★★	★★★★	★★	★★	★★
Barbus cummingi	★★	★★★★	★	★★	★
Barbus everetti Clown Barb	★★	★	★★★	★★	★★★
Barbus hexazona	★★	★★★★	★	★★	★
Barbus lateristriga Tee Barb	★★	★	★★★	★★	★★★
Barbus nigrofasciatus Ruby Barb	★★	★★★★	★★	★★	★★
Barbus oligolepis	★★	★★★★	★	★★	★
Barbus phutunio Dwarf Barb	★★	★★★★	★	★★	★
Barbus schuberti Golden Barb	★★	★★★★	★★	★★	★★
Barbus tetrazona Tiger Barb	★★★	★	★★	★★	★
Barbus titteya Cherry Barb	★	★★★★	★	★★	★
Betta splendens Siamese Fighting Fish (Male)	★	★★	★	★★	★
(Female)	★	★	★	★★	★

	Tendency to School	Community Fish	Required Tank Size	Breeding Habits	Size of Adults
Black Mollienisia	★	★★★★	★★	★	★
Botia macracantha Clown Loach	★★	★★★	★★	★★★	★★
Brachydanio albolineatus Pearl Danio	★★★	★★★★	★	★★	★
Brachydanio nigrofasciatus Spotted Danio	★★★	★★★★	★	★★	★
Brachydanio rerio Zebra Danio	★★★	★★★★	★	★★	★
Brachygobius xanthozonus Bumblebee	★	★★★	★	★★	★
Callichthys callichthys Bubble Nesting Catfish	★	★★★★	★★	★★★	★★
Carnegiella marthae Crystal Hatchet Fish	★	★★★	★	★★★	★
Carnegiella strigata Marble Hatchet Fish	★	★★★	★	★★★	★
Cheirodon axelrodi Cardinal Tetra	★	★★★★	★	★★	★
Chilodus punctatus Pearl Head-stander	★	★★	★★	★★★	★★
Cichlasoma festivum Flag Cichlid	★	★	★★★	★★	★★★
Cichlasoma meeki Fire-mouth	★	★	★★★	★★	★★
Cichlasoma nigrofasciatum Kongo Cichlid	★	★	★★★	★★	★★★
Cichlasoma severum Convict Fish	★	★	★★★	★★	★★★

	Tendency to School	Community Fish	Required Tank Size	Breeding Habits	Size of Adults
Colisa fasciata Giant Gourami	★	★★★★	★★	★★	★★
Colisa labiosa Thick-lipped Gourami	★	★★★★	★	★★	★
Colisa lalia Dwarf Gourami	★	★★★★	★	★★	★
Copeina arnoldi	★	★★★	★	★★	★
Copeina guttata	★	★★★	★★	★★★	★★
Corydoras aeneus Bronze Catfish	★	★★★★	★	★★	★
Corydoras hastatus Midget Catfish	★	★★★★	★	★★★	★
Corydoras julii Leopard Catfish	★	★★★★	★	★★★	★
Corydoras melanistius Spotted Catfish	★	★★★★	★	★★★	★
Corydoras paleatus	★	★★★★	★	★★	★
Cynolebias bellottii Argentine Pearl Fish	★	★★★	★	★★★	★
Danio malabaricus Giant Danio	★★★	★	★★★	★★	★★★
Dermogenys pusillus Half Beak	★	★★★	★	★	★
Epiplatys chaperi Panchax Chaperi	★	★★★	★	★★	★
Etroplus maculatus Orange Chromide	★	★★★★	★★	★★	★★
Exodon paradoxus	★	★	★★	★★★	★★

	Tendency to School	Community Fish	Required Tank Size	Breeding Habits	Size of Adults
Gasteropelecus levis Silver Hatchet Fish	★	★★★	★	★★★	★
Geophagus jurupari Earth Eater	★	★	★★★	★★	★★★
Gymnocorymbus ternetzi Black Tetra	★★	★★★★	★★	★★	★
Gymnotus carapo Brown Knife Fish	★	★	★★★	★★★	★★★
Haplochromis multicolor Egyptian Mouthbreeder	★	★	★	★★	★
Helostoma temmincki Kissing Gourami	★	★★	★★	★★	★★★
Hemichromis bimaculatus Jewel Fish	★	★	★★★	★★	★★
Hemigrammus caudovittatus Tetra von Buenos Aires	★★	★	★★	★★	★★
Hemigrammus erythrozonus Formerly and incorrectly *Hyphessobrycon gracilis* Glow Light Tetra	★★	★★★★	★	★★	★
Hemigrammus nanus Silver Tip Tetra	★★	★★★★	★	★★	★
Hemigrammus ocellifer Head and Tail Light	★★★	★★★★	★	★★	★
Hemigrammus pulcher Rasbora Tetra	★★	★★★★	★	★★	★
Hemigrammus rhodostomus Rummy Nose Tetra	★★★	★★★★	★	★★	★
Heterandria formosa Mosquito Fish	★	★★★★	★	★	★
Hyphessobrycon callistus Tetra Minor Tetra Serpae	★★★	★★★★	★	★★	★

	Tendency to School	Community Fish	Required Tank Size	Breeding Habits	Size of Adults
Hyphessobrycon eos Dawn Tetra	★★	★★★★	★	★★	★
Hyphessobrycon flammeus Flame Tetra Tetra von Rio	★★★	★★★★	★	★★	★
Hyphessobrycon heterorhabdus Tetra Ulreyi	★★	★★★★	★	★★	★
Hyphessobrycon innesi Neon Tetra	★★★	★★★★	★	★★	★
Hyphessobrycon pulchripinnis Lemon Tetra	★★	★★★★	★	★★	★
Hyphessobrycon rosaceus Rosy Tetra	★★	★★★★	★	★★	★
Hyphessobrycon scholzei Black Line Tetra	★★	★	★★	★★	★★
Jordanella floridae American Flag Fish	★	★	★	★★	★
Kryptopterus bicirrhus Glass Catfish	★★	★★★	★	★★★	★★
Lebistes reticulatus Guppy	★	★★★★	★	★	★
Leporinus fasciatus	★	★★	★★★	★★★	★★★
Limia nigrofasciata Hump Backed Limia	★	★★★★	★	★	★
Loricaria parva Alligator Catfish	★	★★★★	★	★★★	★★
Macropodus opercularis Paradise Fish	★	★	★	★★	★★
Melanotaenia mccullochi Queensland Rainbow Fish	★★	★★★★	★	★★	★

	Tendency to School	Community Fish	Required Tank Size	Breeding Habits	Size of Adults
Melanotaenia nigrans Australian Rainbow Fish	★★	★★★★	★★	★★	★★
Metynnis roosevelti Silver Dollar	★	★★★	★★	★★★	★★
Mollienisia latipinna Green Sailfin Molly	★	★★★★	★★★	★	★★
Mollienisia sphenops Blue Molly ⎫ individual Sphenop Molly ⎬ color Liberty Molly ⎭ variations	★	★★★★	★★	★	★
Monodactylus argenteus Singapore Angel	★	★★★	★★	★★★	★★
Nannostomus anomalus	★	★★★★	★	★★	★
Nannostomus marginatus	★	★★★★	★	★★	★
Nannostomus trifasciatus	★	★★★★	★	★★	★
Oryzias javanicus Lantern Eyes	★	★★★★	★	★★	★
Oryzias latipes Medaka—Rice Fish	★	★★★★	★	★★	★
Otocinclus affinis Golden Otocinclus	★	★★★★	★	★★★	★
Pantodon buchholzi Butterfly Fish	★	★★★	★★	★★★	★★
Pelmatochromis kribensis African Dwarf Cichlid	★	★★★★	★	★★	★★
Plecostomus plecostomus Sucker-mouth Catfish	★	★★★★	★★	★★★	★★★
Poecilobrycon auratus Pencil Fish	★	★★★★	★	★★	★
Poecilobrycon unifasciatus Red-tail Pencil Fish	★	★★★★	★	★★	★

	Tendency to School	Community Fish	Required Tank Size	Breeding Habits	Size of Adults
Pristella riddlei	★	★★★★	★	★★	★
Pterophyllum scalare Angel Fish	★	★★★★	★★★	★★	★★
Rasbora heteromorpha Red Rasbora	★★	★★★★	★	★★	★
Rasbora maculata	★★	★★★	★	★★	★
Rasbora trilineata Scissors Tail	★★	★★★★	★	★★	★
Rivulus cylindraceus Green Rivulus	★	★★★	★	★★	★
Scatophagus argus *Scatophagus rubrifons* Scats	★	★★★	★★★	★★★	★★
Symphysodon discus Pompadour Fish Disc Cichlid	★	★★★	★★★	★★★	★★★
Thayeria obliqua Penguin Fish	★★	★★★★	★	★★★	★
Tilapia macrocephala African mouthbreeder	★	★	★★★	★★	★★★
Trichogaster leeri Pearl Gourami Mosaic Gourami	★	★★★★	★★	★★	★★
Trichogaster trichopterus Blue Gourami	★	★	★★	★★	★★
Xiphophorus helleri Swordtail	★	★★★★	★★	★	★★
Xiphophorus maculatus Platy Moon					
Xiphophorus variatus Platy Variatus	★	★★★★	★	★	★

All About
Aquariums